The Masonic Book Club

Vol. 8

Samuel Prichard's Masonry Dissected, 1730

Harry Carr

Westphalia Press
An Imprint of the Policy Studies Organization
Washington, DC

SAMUEL PRICHARD'S MASONRY DISSECTED, 1730

All Rights Reserved © 2025 by Policy Studies Organization

Westphalia Press
An imprint of Policy Studies Organization
1367 Connecticut Avenue NW
Washington, D.C. 20036
info@ipsonet.org

ISBN: 978-1-63723-537-9

Daniel Gutierrez-Sandoval, Executive Director
PSO and Westphalia Press

Updated material and comments on this edition
can be found at the Westphalia Press website:
www.westphaliapress.org

The Masonic Book Club

The *Masonic Book Club* (MBC) was formed in 1970 by two Illinois Masons, Alphonse Cerza, 33°, and Louis L. Williams, 33°. The MBC primarily reprinted out-of-print Masonic books with scholarly introductions; occasionally they would print additional texts as "bonuses" (though none were marked specifically as such on the title pages); sometimes a reprint would be marked "Masonic Book Club Edition"; often an unnumbered bonus was published jointly with the Illinois Lodge of Research or the Supreme Council, 33°, NMJ, USA.

Most of the MBC volumes indicated on the title page, "Volume [*Number*] of the Publications of the Masonic Book Club," some were misnumbered, and some were unnumbered. Indeed, the numbering of the early volumes was inconsistent. For example, *A Serious and Impartial Enquiry* is "Volume Five" (1974) but *Masonic Membership of the Founding Fathers* is "The Masonic Book Club Edition" (1974). Then, *Masonry Dissected* is "Volume Eight" (1977), *The Trestleboard* is "Volume 8A" (1978), and *Anderson's Constitutions of 1738* is "Volume Nine" (1978). If nothing else, MBC books keep bibliophiles on their toes.

The first volumes had deckle-edged paper and pages of slightly different sizes, though eventually the MBC settled into a 6"×9" trimmed-page format for their books. The books were bound in a dark blue fabric with gold lettering. Listed below are the fifty-nine MBC volumes published 1970–2010 with bonuses. N.B.: A number and letter, e.g. "Volume 8A," is a numbering for this reprint series.

The club originally was limited to 333 members, but the number grew to nearly 2,000, with 1,083 members when it dissolved in 2010. In 2017 MW Barry Weer, 33°, the last president of the MBC, transferred the MBC name and assets to the Supreme Council, 33°, SJ, USA. Under the editorship of Arturo de Hoyos, 33°, G∴C∴, and S. Brent Morris, 33°, G∴C∴, the revived Masonic Book Club has the goal of publishing classic Masonic books while supporting Scottish Rite, SJ, USA philanthropies.

Publications of the Masonic Book Club, 1970–2010

1	1970	*The Regius Poem*	Masonic Book Club
2	1971	*The Constitutions of the Free-Masons*	Benjamin Franklin
3	1972	*Ahiman Rezon*	Laurence Dermott
4	1973	*Illustrations of Masonry*	William Preston
5	1974	*A Serious and Impartial Enquiry into the Cause of the Present Decay of Free-Masonry in the Kingdom of Ireland*	Fifield D'Assigny
5A	1974*	*Masonic Membership of the Founding Fathers*	Ronald E. Heaton

6	1975	*The Signers of the Declaration of Independence*	David C. Whitney
7	1976	*The Signers of the Constitution of the United States*	David C. Whitney
7A	1976*	*Masonic Symbols in American Decorative Art*	Louis L. Williams & Alphonse Cerza
8	1977	*Samuel Prichard's Masonry Dissected, 1730*	Harry Carr
8A	1978*	*Trestle-Board (A facsimile of the original Trestle Board by the Baltimore Masonic Convention of 1843)*	Dwight L. Smith
9	1978	*Anderson's Constitutions of 1738*	Lewis Edward & W. J. Hughan
10	1979	*Sufferings of John Coustos*	Wallace McLeod
11	1980	*The Revelations of a Square*	George Oliver
11A	1980	*Biblical Characters in Freemasonry*	John H. Van Gorden
11B	1980*	*A Masonic Reader's Guide*	*Guide* Alphonse Cerza & Thomas Warden
12	1981	*Three Distinct Knocks and Jachin and Boaz*	Harry Carr
13	1982	*Masonic Almanacs and Anti-Masonic Almanacs*	Plez A. Transou
13A	1982*	*Stephen A. Douglas: Freemason*	Wayne C. Temple
14	1983	*The Beginnings of Freemasonry in America*	Melvin M. Johnson
14A	1983*	*Bespangled, Painted & Embroidered: Decorated Masonic Aprons in America, 1790–1850*	Scottish Rite Masonic Museum & Library
14B	1983*	*Making a Mason at Sight*	Louis L. Williams
15	1984	*Masonic Concordance of the Holy Bible*	Charles Clyde Hunt
15A	1984*	*By Square and Compasses: The Building of Lincoln's Home and Its Saga*	Wayne C. Temple

16	1985	*The Old Gothic Constitutions*	Wallace McLeod
16A	1985*	*Modern Historical Characters in Freemasonry*	John H. Van Gorden
17	1986	*The Rise and Development of Organised Freemasonry*	Roy A. Wells
17A	1986*	*Ancient and Early Medieval Historical Characters in Freemasonry*	John H. Van Gorden
18	1987	*The Lodge in Friendship Village and Other Stories*	P. W. George
18A	1987*	*Masonic Charities*	John H. Van Gorden & Stewart M. L. Pollard
18B	1987*	*Medieval Historical Characters in Freemasonry*	John H. Van Gorden
18C	1987*	*George Washington in New York*	Allan Boudreau & Alexander Bleimann
19	1988	*Records of the Hole Crafte and Fellowship of Masons*	Edward Conder, Jr.
20	1989	*A Candid Disquisition of the Principles and Practices of the Most Ancient and Honourable Society of Free and Accepted Masons*	Wellins Calcott
20A	1989*	*Freemasonry and Nauvoo, 1839–1846*	Robin L. Carr
21	1990	*Masonic Odes and Poems*	Rob Morris
22	1991	*Lessing's Masonic Dialogues*	Gotthold Lessing
22A	1991*	*ABC of Freemasonry: A Book for Beginners*	Delmar D. Darrah
23	1992	*The Folger Manuscript*	S. Brent Morris
24	1993	*Freemasonry and Christianity: Lectures from Two Ages*	T. De Witt Peake & John J. Murchison
25	1994	*The Constitutions of St. John's Lodge*	Robin L. Carr
25A	1994*	*The Mystic Tie and Men of Letters*	Robin L. Carr
26	1995	*Recollections of a Masonic Veteran*	S. Brent Morris

27	1996	*The Freemason's Monitor or Illustrations of Masonry in Two Parts*	Thomas Smith Webb
28	1997	*The Masonic Ladder or the Nine Steps to Ancient Freemasonry*	John Sherer
28A	1997*	*Freemasonry and Democracy: Its Evolution in North America*	Allen E. Roberts & Wallace McLeod
29	1998	*The Masonic Harp: Collection of Masonic Odes, Hymns, Songs*	George Wingate Chase
30	1999	*Symbolic Teachings of Masonry and Its Message*	Thomas Milton Stewart
31	2000	*Freemasonry Its Meaning and Significance, An Exposition of its Ethics, Religion and Philosophy*	Otto Caspari
32	2001	*K. R. Cama Masonic Jubilee Volume*	Jivanji Jamshedji Modi
33	2002	*Caementaria Hibernica*	W. J. Chetwode Crawley
34	2003	*A Daily Advancement in Masonic Knowledge*	Wallace McLeod & S. Brent Morris
35	2004	*The Craftsman, and Templar's Textbook and, also, Melodies for the Craft*	Cornelius Moore
36	2005	*The Text Book of Freemasonry*	Retired Member of the Craft
37	2006	*Orations of the Illustrious Brother Frederick Dalcho Esq., M.D.*	Frederick Dalcho
38	2007	*Antiquities of Freemasonry Comprising Illustrations of the Five Grand Periods of Masonry from the Creation of the World to the Dedication of King Solomon's Temple*	George Oliver
39	2008	*Diogenes' Lamp or an Examination of our Present-Day Morality and Enlightenment*	Adam Weishaupt
40	2009	*Proofs of Conspiracy Against All the Governments of Europe*	John Robison
41	2010	*The Evolution of Freemasonry*	Delmar Darrah

* indicates a bonus book

Samuel Prichard's Masonry Dissected, 1730

SAMUEL PRICHARD'S
Masonry Dissected
1730

Harry Carr

SAMUEL PRICHARD'S
Masonry Dissected
1730

An Analysis and Commentary
by
Harry Carr

VOLUME EIGHT
of the publications of
THE MASONIC BOOK CLUB

Published by
THE MASONIC BOOK CLUB
A Not-for-Profit Corporation of Illinois
Bloomington, Illinois
1977

[This appeared in the original printing]

This volume has been published solely for the Members of The Masonic Book Club and is limited to 999 copies of which this is

No. 407

© 1977, by The Masonic Book Club
Printed in the United States of America

CONTENTS

INTRODUCTION

BIBLIOGRAPHICAL NOTES	3
The Four Advertisements	4
SAMUEL PRICHARD—HIS MASONIC BACKGROUND	7
The Old Charges in Prichard's Day	11
The Three Clues	12
Accepted Masonry	16
The Author's Vindication of Himself	18
MASONIC CATECHISMS AND EXPOSURES	20
The 'Haughfoot Fragment'	21
Stages in the Evaluation of Catechisms & Exposures	23
Masonry Dissected—The Text of the Exposure	26
THE FIRST HIRAMIC LEGEND—SOURCES	29
THE EVOLUTION OF THE THREE-DEGREE SYSTEM	34
MASONRY DISSECTED—ITS INFLUENCE ON THE RITUAL	43

THE FACSIMILE   45

NOTES

THE ENTER'D 'PRENTICE'S DEGREE	79
Test Questions	79
A Just and Perfect Lodge	80
Preparation of the Candidate	80
Perambulation	81
Posture for the Obligation	81
The Obligation	82
Form and Dimensions of the Lodge	84
Location and Orientation of the Lodge	85
Three Pillars—Wisdom, Strength and Beauty	86

Furniture & Jewels	86
Lights & Fix'd Lights	87
Situations & Duties of the Officers	88
Secrets—The Tongue of Good Report	88
Geometry	88
Principal Signs	89
Miscellaneous Questions	89
Two Pillars for the E.A.—Lettering	90
Miscellaneous Questions	91
The Fellow Craft's Degree	92
The F.C. Catechism	94
Geometry and the Letter G	94
Travel, Work, Wages.—The Middle Chamber	95
The Pillars—Their Dimensions & Ornamentation	96
Tests for Admission to the Middle Chamber	96
Religious Significance of the Letter G	97
Geometry Again	98
A Greeting	98
The F.C. Pillar	99
The Master's Degree	101
God and The Square	101
The Essence of the Third Degree	104
Doggerel Verse	104
The Rule of Three	105
The Keys of all Lodges	105
M.B.	106
Lost and is now found	106
Emblem on Front Cover	108
Colophon	109

LIST OF ABBREVIATED REFERENCES

A.Q.C.	*Ars Quatuor Coronatorum* [Transactions of the Quatuor Coronati Lodge, No. 2076, London.]
B.of C.	*Book of Constitutions.*
C.C.MS.	*Chetwode-Crawley MS.*, c.1700.
'Edinburgh Group'	*The Edinburgh Register House MS.*, and its sister texts, the *Chetwode-Crawley* and the *Kevan MSS.*
E.F.E.	*The Early French Exposures*, published by the Q.C. Lodge.
E.M.C.	*The Early Masonic Catechisms*, by Knoop, Jones and Hamer, 2nd. edition, published by the Q.C.Lodge.
E.R.H.MS.	*The Edinburgh Register House MS.*, 1696.
J.& B.	*Jachin and Boaz*, 1762.
Q.C.A.	*Quatuor Coronatorum Antigrapha* [Masonic Reprints of the Q.C.Lodge].
T.D.K.	*Three Distinct Knocks*, 1760.
Trahi	*L'Ordre des Francs-Maçons Trahi*, 1745.

PREFACE

Masonry Dissected, by Samuel Prichard, first published in 1730, was an easy book to select for publication by The Masonic Book Club for it has been a Masonic classic for many years. The book has been out-of-print for many years and has been hard to locate even in Masonic libraries. It was the first major exposé of the Masonic ritual to be printed; and it occupies an important place in the history of the ritual because it contains the first clear description of a system of three degrees.

We were fortunate in securing the assistance of Brother Harry Carr, a Past Master of Quatuor Coronati Lodge, and one of the greatest living Masonic scholars, in writing the Introduction to the background of the subject with notes covering the possible sources of specific parts of the Prichard book.

Brother Carr's careful research permits him to present all that is known about the author of the book. Prichard's work attracted immediate attention and many editions were published within a short period of time. It became a "best seller" of its day and soon there were several pirated editions. Harry Carr has been a student of the history of the Masonic ritual for many years, and his experience is reflected in the detailed explanation of the Prichard book, the sources of his material, its influence on the ritual of his day and on the English and European exposures in the next fifty years. Undoubtedly, Prichard had some knowledge of the Ancient Constitutions, and this phase of the subject is explored in detail by Brother Carr, together with the available literature on the subject. One interesting part of the book is that Brother Carr explores all the ways and by-ways of each factor involved in the subject, with ample references to available studies made by others. The explanation sheds valuable light on many phases of the history of Masonic ritual. The student of Freemasonry will find the reading and studying of this book an intellectual adventure because of the presentation of the material by Brother Harry Carr. It will be a welcome addition to any Masonic library, and we are proud to make this rare book available to our members.

Harry Carr was born in 1900, and at an early age won a scholarship to Davenant Foundation School in England. At the age of fourteen he started to work in a retail store and at the age of nineteen he joined his father in business. In World War II he was a Lance-Corporal in the Royal Berkshire Home Guard stationed at Newbury. He was successful in business and was able to retire in 1961 to devote his full time to the study of Freemasonry.

In 1929 he was initiated in Barnato Lodge No. 2265, and served the lodge as Worshipful Master in 1943. He was exalted in Barnato Chapter in 1935, and reached the Chair in 1945. He helped form other lodges and for many years he was Secretary for two lodges. In the year 1936 he joined Barnato Lodge of Instruction and read his first paper before that lodge the same year. He became active in several other research lodges. He was appointed to London Grand Rank in 1953, with subsequent Grand Rank promotions in 1960 and 1969. His earliest Masonic writings were published by the Leicester Lodge of Research from 1943 onwards. In 1938 he joined the Correspondence Circle of Quatuor Coronati Lodge, and was elected a full member of the lodge in 1953. In 1957 he was honoured by the Grand Lodge appointment as Prestonian Lecturer for that year, and he served the Quatuor Coronati as Worshipful Master in 1959. Later he was to render outstanding service to that lodge as Secretary and Editor of its Transactions, and is credited with attracting many new members to the lodge by the excellence of the Transactions published during the time that he was Editor.

As a Masonic scholar Brother Carr has no peer. His first paper appeared in the Transactions of Quatuor Coronati Lodge in 1950-1951. He has been the author of many papers that have appeared in these Transactions and has been instrumental in the publication of a collection of the twelve earliest French Exposures of the ritual, 1737-1751, all translated into English: *The Minutes of the Lodge of Edinburgh, (Mary's Chapel) No. 1* starting with the year 1598; and *The Minutes of Lodge Mother Kilwinning, No. 0*, starting with the year 1642. His latest book, *The Freemason at Work*, contains two hundred questions and answers selected from letters received by him during the time he was Editor of the Transactions. He is best known in the United States for his illuminating and interesting lectures on the History of the Masonic ritual delivered here during many tours in recent years.

ALPHONSE CERZA
LOUIS L. WILLIAMS

SAMUEL PRICHARD'S

Masonry Dissected

1730

INTRODUCTION

BIBLIOGRAPHICAL NOTES[1]

The first edition of this 32 pp. 8vo. pamphlet (approx. 7⅝" × 4½") was advertised for sale in a London newspaper, the *Daily Journal*, on Tuesday, 20 October 1730:

> This day is published . . . MASONRY DISSECTED . . . by Samuel Prichard . . . Printed for J. Wilford . . .

The second edition was advertised the very next day, 21 October, and again on the 23rd, two days later: the third edition was advertised on Saturday, 31 October 1730, and these two editions were also printed for Wilford. (See advertisements on pp. 4, 5.)

Meanwhile the pamphlet had been reprinted in *Read's Weekly Journal or British Gazetteer*, on Saturday 24 October 1730. This was apparently a pirated version in which the whole thirty-one printed pages of the original were crammed into two pages of the newspaper, each approximately 15" × 10".

Another pirated edition, dated MD.CC.XXX. printed by Thomas Nichols, 'without Temple Bar' (London) had also probably made its appearance by the end of October 1730.

Prichard's text was reprinted, in two parts, in separate issues of the *Northampton Mercury*, the first section, up to the end of the Enter'd 'Prentice's Degree, in October 1730, and the remainder, from the Fellow-Craft's Degree to the end, on 2 November 1730.

Thus, there were three separate editions by Prichard, and a pirated edition (Nichols), plus a newspaper version (Read's) all

Continued on page 6.

---

[1] In compiling the notes under this heading, I am much indebted to three specialist studies: (1) *The Early Masonic Catechisms*, by Knoop, Jones and Hamer, 2nd edition, pp. 157/8: (2) "Prichard's *Masonry Dissected*", by Comdr. S. N. Smith, *A.Q.C. 51* pp. 138/9: (3) John T. Thorp, in *Leicester Lodge of Research Masonic Reprints*, Vol. XII (1929) pp. 10/11 [H.C.]

The *Daily Journal*, Tuesday, 20 October 1730

> **This Day is Publiſhed,**
> *(Dedicated to the Right Worſhipful and Honourable Fraternity of Free and Accepted Maſons, and the Author's Affidavit before Sir Richard Hopkins prefix'd)*
> MASONRY DISSECTED: Being a Univerſal and Genuine Deſcription of all its Branches, from the Original to this Preſent Time; as it deliver'd in the Conſtituted Regular Lodges both in City and Country, according to the feveral Degrees of Admiſſion. Giving an Impartial Account of their Regular Proceeding in Initiating their New-Members in the whole Three Degrees of Maſonry, viz. I. Enter'd Apprentice. II. Fellow Craft. III. Maſter. To which is added, The Author's Vindication of himſelf. By SAMUEL PRITCHARD, late Member of a Conſtituted Lodge.
> Printed for J. WILFORD, at the Three Flower-de-Luces behind the Chapter-Houſe, near St. Paul's. Price 6 d.

The first advertisement.

The *Daily Journal*, Wednesday, 21 October 1730

> **This Day is Publiſhed,**
> *(Dedicated to the Right Worſhipful and Honourable Fraternity of Free and Accepted Maſons, and the Author's Affidavit before Sir Richard Hopkins prefix'd)*
> *The SECOND EDITION, of*
> MASONRY DISSECTED: Being a Univerſal and Genuine Deſcription of all its Branches, from the Original to this Preſent Time; as it deliver'd in the Conſtituted Regular Lodges both in City and Country, according to the feveral Degrees of Admiſſion. Giving an Impartial Account of their Regular Proceeding in Initiating their New-Members in the whole Three Degrees of Maſonry, viz. I. Enter'd Apprentice. II. Fellow Craft. III. Maſter. To which is added, The Author's Vindication of himſelf. By SAMUEL PRITCHARD, late Member of a Conſtituted Lodge.
> Printed for J. WILFORD, at the Three Flower-de-Luces behind the Chapter-Houſe, near St. Paul's. Price 6 d.

The second advertisement. "The Second Edition of" has been inserted after line 4.

The *Daily Journal*, Friday, 23 October 1730

> **This Day is Publiſhed,**
> *(Dedicated to the Right Worſhipful and Honourable Fraternity of Free and Accepted Maſons,*
> The SECOND EDITION, of
> MASONRY DISSECTED: Being a Univerſal and Genuine Deſcription of all its Branches, from the Original to this Preſent Time; as it deliver'd in the Conſtituted Regular Lodges both in City and Country, according to the ſeveral Degrees of Admiſſion. Giving an Impartial Account of their Regular Proceeding in Initiating their New-Members in the whole Three Degrees of Maſonry, viz. I. Enter'd Apprentice. II. Fellow Craft. III. Maſter. To which is added, The Author's Vindication of himſelf. By SAMUEL PRITCHARD, late Member of a Conſtituted Lodge.
> Printed for J. WILFORD, at the Three Flower-de-Luces behind the Chapter-Houſe, near St. Paul's. Price 6 d.
> N. B. There is prefixed to this Account, a True Copy of the Affidavit made before Sir RICHARD HOPKINS, of its Truth and Genuineneſs in every Particular, without which all other Accounts are ſpurious, and groſs Impoſitions on the Publick.

The third advertisement. Original lines 4 and 5 are omitted and a footnote is added.

The *Daily Journal*, Saturday, 31 October 1730

> **This Day is Publiſhed,**
> *(With a Liſt of the Regular Lodges, according to their Seniority and Conſtitution)*
> The THIRD EDITION, of
> MASONRY DISSECTED: Being a Univerſal and Genuine Deſcription of all its Branches, from the Original to this Preſent Time; as it is deliver'd in the Conſtituted Regular Lodges both in City and Country, according to the ſeveral Degrees of Admiſſion. Giving an Impartial Account of their Regular Proceeding in Initiating their New-Members in the whole Three Degrees of Maſonry, viz. I. Enter'd Apprentice. II. Fellow Craft. III. Maſter. To which is added, The Author's Vindication of himſelf. By SAMUEL PRITCHARD, late Member of a Conſtituted Lodge.
> Printed for J. WILFORD, at the Three Flower-de-Luces behind the Chapter-Houſe, near St. Paul's. Price 6 d.
> N. B. There is prefixed to this Account, a True Copy of the Affidavit made before Sir RICHARD HOPKINS, of its Truth and Genuineneſs in every Particular, without which all other Accounts are ſpurious, and groſs Impoſitions on the Publick.

The fourth advertisement. 'Third' instead of 'Second' and the word 'is', previously omitted, is now added in line 6.

printed in London, and a two-part newspaper version, printed in the Midlands, all within fourteen days!

Thorp, writing in 1929, listed another fourteen editions before 1760 and nine more before the end of the 18th century. Bro. Knoop and his collaborators, writing in 1943, mentioned 'thirty numbered editions . . . printed in England, and eight . . . in Scotland'.

In spite of this seeming profusion of copies, all the earlier editions are scarce and the four versions dated 1730 are extremely rare. There is a copy of the first edition in the Library of the United Grand Lodge of England and one in the Library of the Grand Lodge of Massachusetts. Another first edition (formerly in the Wallace Heaton collection) is now owned by the present writer. There is a copy of the second edition in the Leicester Masonic Library (reprinted by J. T. Thorp in 1929). The third edition is the earliest in the British Museum collection. That version was the first to contain 'A List of Regular Lodges according to their Seniority and Constitution' and it was reproduced by Bro. Douglas Knoop and his colleagues in *The Early Masonic Catechisms*, 1943. The excellent collection in the Library of the Grand Lodge of Massachusetts also includes a copy of the Nichols pirated print.

SAMUEL PRICHARD
His Masonic Background

Among the many characters who made their mark in Masonic history during the early decades of the first Grand Lodge, Samuel Prichard must surely rank as one of the most extraordinary. As a person, nothing is known about him, his family, social status, trade, or profession; he remains a complete mystery.

In October 1730 he published *Masonry Dissected*, a very successful pamphlet which claimed to be 'A Universal and Genuine Description of [Masonry in] all its Branches'. At the next Quarterly Communication of Grand Lodge on 15 December 1730 he was roundly condemned as 'an Impostor':

> The Deputy Grand Master took notice of a Pamphlet lately published by one Pritchard [*sic*] who pretends to have been made a regular Mason: In Violation of the Obligation of a Mason wch he swears he has broke in order to do hurt to Masonry and expressing himself with the utmost Indignation against both him (stiling him an Impostor) and of his Book as a foolish thing not to be regarded. But in order to prevent the Lodges being imposed upon by false Brethren or Impostors: Proposed . . . that no Person whatsoever should be admitted into Lodges unless some Member of the Lodge then present would vouch for such visiting Brothers being a regular Mason, and the Member's Name to be entred against the Visitor's Name in the Lodge Book, which Proposal was unanimously agreed to. (*Q.C.A.* X, pp. 135/6).

This was the only occasion on which Prichard's name appeared in the Grand Lodge Minutes. His Lodge was not mentioned and, so far as official records go, it is not even certain that he had ever been admitted into the Craft.

The only information to be found about him is that which can be deduced from his book as a whole, but especially from the eight preliminary pages, and from *'The Author's Vindication of himself . . .'*, which formed its final chapter. The sources from which these details can be gathered are of two kinds:

(a) Direct statements, made by Prichard, about himself and his reasons for compiling the book.
(b) Inferences that may properly be drawn from the knowledge of the Craft that he displayed in his introductory pages and in the text of his exposure.

There is reason to believe that the information thus obtained may furnish useful light on Prichard as a Mason and on his capacity as a writer on Masonry, all the more valuable, perhaps, because of the total absence of other sources. In the following notes the page numbers shown in [ ] refer to un-numbered pages in the first edition of *Masonry Dissected*.

LATE MEMBER OF A CONSTITUTED LODGE: [p. I]. Prichard's claim that he was *'late Member of a CONSTITUTED LODGE'* implies that he was a Mason who had resigned or been excluded. This was probably true. Quite apart from his ritual text (which does not necessarily prove that he had been a Mason) there is evidence to show that he had a very good knowledge of Masonry and its background, and there is no reason to doubt his claim.

There is indeed a record of a 'Mr Sam^1. Pritchard' in the minutes of the Lodge held at the Swan and Rummer Tavern, in Finch Lane, London, showing that he was a visitor to that Lodge on 25 September 1728, and the record also mentions his Lodge. It runs:

'Mr. Sam^1. Pritchard [of] Harry ye
8th head 7 Dyalls'
                                    (Hughan, *A.Q.C.* 10, p.134).

The names Prichard and Pritchard are interchangeable, and this entry may have been made by the Secretary of the Lodge, who included the 't'. Grand Lodge also used the spelling 'Pritchard' in the minutes of 15 December 1730, above, and it appeared so in the advertisements, but not in Prichard's book.

Little is known about the Lodge at 'King Henry ye VIII Head' except that it was a 'Regular Constituted Lodge', and was so recorded in the Grand Lodge List for 25 November 1725[2] when it had seventeen members whose names are also recorded (but Prichard's name was not among them). The Lodge sent representatives, Master and Wardens, to the Quarterly Communications in June 1728 and in December 1730[3], after which it seems to have disappeared.

If we could be sure that the visitor to the Swan and Rummer on 25 September 1728 was *our* Samuel Prichard, the record would be doubly interesting, partly because we know that the Lodge had a number of distinguished visitors, but chiefly because it was one of the earliest English Lodges recorded as working the third degree. Needless to say, Prichard's chief claim to Masonic fame or notoriety was his publication of *Masonry Dissected*, the first exposure of the ritual of three degrees.

The word 'CONSTITUTED', on Prichard's title-page, had a special significance at that time. The first *Book of Constitutions*, 1723, contained a chapter describing 'the Manner of constituting a New Lodge' and on 25 November 1723 the Grand Lodge had ruled:

> That no new Lodge in or near London without it be regularly Constituted be Countenanced by the Grand Lodge, nor the Ma^r or Wardens admitted at the Grand Lodge.[4]

Prichard's use of the word 'Constituted' was intended to emphasize the regularity of his former Lodge, but it may well indicate a better than average knowledge of what was going on in the Grand Lodge.

THE OATH: [p. II]. A greatly inferior exposure, *The Mystery of Free-Masonry*, had been on sale in London under various titles, since August 1730. Prichard's work was infinitely better and he probably decided to use the Oath as a plain piece of salesmanship, guaranteeing the quality of his own publication. It was sworn, before a magistrate, Sir Richard Hopkins, an Alderman of the Lime Street Ward of the City of London, on 13 October 1730.

It seems that pirated versions, under the same title, had begun to appear immediately after Prichard's first edition came out on Oc-

---

[2] *Minutes of the Grand Lodge . . . 1723-1739*, Q.C.A. X, p. 43.

[3] *ibid*, pp. 86, 133.

[4] *ibid*, p. 54.

tober 20, and he altered the October 23 advertisement for his second edition, by inserting a note which referred to the Oath (or Affidavit):

> N.B. There is prefixed to this Account, a True Copy of the Affidavit made before Sir Richard Hopkins, of its Truth and Genuineness in every Particular, without which all other accounts are spurious and gross Impositions on the Publick . . .

THE DEDICATION: [pp. III, IV]. This was addressed to the Fraternity itself, in polite and respectful terms, but when read in conjunction with the 'Author's Vindication of himself' at the end of the work, the dedication appears to be tinged with irony.

Masonry Dissected: pp. 5-8. In this section, Prichard compared 'the original Institution of Masonry' with the 'Accepted Masonry' of his own day. He began with a very brief précis of the story of the Craft, as told (with many variations) in practically every version of the *Old Charges* or *MS. Constitutions.* He mentioned 'the Liberal Arts and Sciences; but more especially . . . *Geometry*' and traced the transmission of 'the Art and Mystery of Masonry' from 'the Building of the Tower of Babel', through Euclid, who

> communicated it to *Hiram*, the Master-Mason concern'd in the Building of *Solomon's* Temple in *Jerusalem*, where was an excellent and curious Mason that was the chief under their Grand-Master *Hiram*, whose Name was *Mannon Grecus*, who taught the Art of Masonry to one *Carolos Marcil in France*, who was afterwards elected King of France, ...

Omitting many details, but still following the *Old Charges* in outline, Prichard noted that the Craft was brought from France and became established in England, where 'Masons were made in the Manner following':

> *Tunc unus ex Senioribus teneat Librum, ut illi vel ille ponant vel ponat Manus supra Librum; tum Praecepta debeant legi.*
> i.e. *Whilst one of the Seniors holdeth the Book, that he or they put their Hands upon the Book, whilst the Master ought to read the Laws or Charges.*

It is obvious that Prichard was well acquainted with one or more versions of the *Old Charges*, although he did not name specific texts; but he did leave several clues, and the search is rewarding, because it produces valuable evidence of his status as a student of Freemasonry.

THE OLD CHARGES IN PRICHARD'S DAY

Some 130 versions of the *Old Charges* have survived to this day, ranging in date from *c.*1390 right through to the mid-18th century. Several of them are copies of earlier versions, but all of them—even the *early copies*—are rare and valuable manuscripts. Modern students are fortunate, because most of them have been reproduced in print during the past hundred years or more, so that their contents are readily accessible nowadays.

In Prichard's day, however, the majority of them would have been stored in private libraries, or in antiquarian collections, out of reach of the public, and their existence in most cases was unknown. There was, nevertheless, a great interest among Masonic leaders in these old documents which purported to recount the history of the Craft since Bible times, together with the Charges or Regulations by which the masons were governed. In the 'historical' section of Anderson's *Book of Constitutions*, 1738, (p. 110) he recorded, for 24 June 1718:

> George Payne Esq: *Grand Master* . . . desired any Brethren to bring to the Grand Lodge any old *Writings* and *Records* concerning *Masons* and *Masonry* in order to shew the Usages of antient Times: And this Year several old Copies of the *Gothic Constitutions* were produced and collated.

On 24 June 1720, at the beginning of Payne's second term as Grand Master, Anderson noted that:

> This Year, at some *private* Lodges, several very valuable *Manuscripts* (for they had nothing yet in Print) concerning the Fraternity, their Lodges, Regulations, Charges, Secrets, and Usages . . . were too hastily burnt by some scrupulous Brothers, that those Papers might not fall into strange Hands. (*ibid* p.111)

At the Grand Festival in June 1721, Payne exhibited the *Cooke MS.*, *c.*1410, (now acknowledged as the second oldest version of the *Old Charges*).

Anderson had said, correctly, that 'they had nothing yet in Print' (in 1720), but this was partially remedied in the next few years. In 1722, a version of the *Old Constitutions* was 'Printed, and Sold by J. Roberts, in *Warwick Lane*' [London].

In 1724, and again in 1725, another pamphlet was 'Printed for Sam. Briscoe, at the Bell-Savage, on *Ludgate-Hill*', and came on sale there and at three other places in London. It is now known as the *Briscoe Pamphlet*, and contains a varied collection of Masonic odds-and-ends including a version of the *Old Charges*.

In 1728/9 Benjamin Cole published another version, in book form; it was printed from engraved plates in three different states and the first 'edition' may have appeared a year or two before 1728. These three versions are *the only texts known to have been in print* at the time when Prichard was preparing to publish his exposure. In addition there were a number of copies of several versions, most of them made by William Reid, who was Grand Secretary from 1727-1734. He was responsible for three texts, now known as the *Fisher MS.*, c.1726; *Songhurst MS.*, c.1726; and the *Spencer MS.*, 1726, all three being virtually identical. Two years later, he produced another version, the *Woodford MS.*, 1728, which was a copy of the *Cooke MS.* of c.1410.

One more text must be added to this list, because it is of special interest, i.e. the *Bolt-Coleraine MS.*, dated 1728, which will be discussed more fully, below.

This completes the list of all the print and manuscript versions of the *Old Charges* that could have been readily accessible to Prichard in the years before he published his *Masonry Dissected*. He may, indeed, have had access to other versions, but that is extremely doubtful because—had they been available—there would almost certainly have been some record of their being copied, as was the case with the *Cooke MS.* and *Songhurst, Spencer, Fisher and Bolt-Coleraine MSS.*

THE THREE CLUES

We may return now to the three clues which Prichard left; they consist of the two names, '*Mannon Grecus*' and '*Carolos Marcil*', with the Latin instruction '*Tunc unus ex Senioribus . . .*' Among the 130 surviving versions of the *Old Charges*, there are many which lack all three items. Some contain one or both names in a fantastic variety of spellings[5], but they omit the Latin instruction; others contain that instruction in English. Only a small proportion contain all three items, i.e., two names with the Latin text, but their spellings differ widely from Prichard's clues. The following extracts, all earlier than 1730, may serve as illustrations, from versions that contain all three 'clues'.

Prichard's words, for comparison	MANNON GRECUS	CAROLOS MARCIL	Latin text (see p. 10 above)
Thorp MS, 1629. AQC.Vol.11. pp.209/210	NAYMUS GREEUS	CHARLES MARTILL	Spellings differ
Beaumont MS.1690 *Yorkshire Old Charges*, pp.76/8 By Poole & Worts	MAMON GRECUS	CARALUS MARCHILL	Spellings differ
Bain MS.1670-1680 AQC. Vol. 20, pp.260,263.	[BLANK] GROECUS	CHARLES MARTELL	Spellings differ
Drinkwater MS.No.1. c.1710 *Trans.Manchester Assn. for Mas. Research*.Vol.XV	MANNON GRAECUM	CAROLUS MARTYLL	Words differ

It is doubtful if Prichard had access to any of these texts, but even if he had, it is clear that none of them could have been his source for those names, or for the Latin instruction.

The manuscript and printed versions of the *Old Charges* that are *known to have been accessible to Prichard before 1730* are equally unhelpful except in one case. As regards the three clues, for which we are searching, they exhibit wide variations of detail, e.g., the *Spencer*, *Songhurst*, and *Fisher MSS.*, and the *Cole* engraved versions have neither the two names nor the Latin instruction. The *Cooke MS.* of c.1410 (and the *Woodford MS.*, which was a copy made in 1728) have only one of the names, given as 'Carolus Secundus', but they lack the Latin passage. The *Briscoe* print of 1724

---

[5] The first name, 'Mannon Grecus' appears in versions ranging from 'Naymus Grecus' to 'Minus Greenatus, alias Green'. The second name 'Carolos Marcil' appears in versions ranging from 'Carolus Martyll' to 'Charles Marshall'.

gives both names 'Nainus Grœcus' and 'Charles Martil', but again the Latin instruction is omitted. The *Roberts* print, of 1722, has both names, with the Latin instruction, but none of the three items matches Prichard's clues, i.e.

Roberts, 1722.   Memongrecus   : Carolus Martel

Masonry Dissected, 1730.   Mannon Grecus: Carolos Marcil

and for the Latin passage:

Roberts, 1722	*Prichard*, 1730
Tunc Unus ex Senioribus veniat Librum illi qui Injurandum reddat & ponat Manum in Libro vel supra librum dum Articulus & Precepta sibi legentur.	*Tunc unus ex Senioribus teneat Librum, ut illi vel ille ponant vel ponat Manus supra Librum; tum Praecepta debeant legi.*

After much searching, there is only one version of the 'Old Charges' that contains all three of Prichard's clues and that can be proved to have been in circulation at the time when Prichard was preparing his material. It is the *Bolt-Coleraine MS.*, dated 1728, and is believed to have been copied by one, William Askew, from an original now lost. This text of 1728 was in a small book of forty-three pages, with an inscription which suggests that it was commissioned by Lord Coleraine, or prepared for presentation to him, at the time when he was Grand Master in 1727/8. The inscription runs:

The Constitutions of the Right Hon[ble]
and Worshipfull Fraternity of Free
and Accepted Masons

A.M.	5728
A.D.	1728

The Rt. Hon[ble] Henry Lord Colerane
Baron of Colerane in the Kingdom of Ireland

Grand Master
Odi Profanum

The book was in the possession of the Bristol Masonic Society until 1941, when it was destroyed by enemy action; fortunately a transcript survived and that was reproduced in full in Gould's *History of Freemasonry* (Poole's edition, 1951, Vol I. pp. 25-29).

As to Prichard's *name* clues, those in *Bolt-Coleraine* are almost, but not quite identical:

| Prichard, 1730 | Mannon Grecus | Carolos Marcil |
| Bolt-Coleraine, 1728 | Mannon Grecus | Carolus Marcill |

As to the Latin instruction, in all except the spelling of one word, the two versions are word-for-word identical:

Prichard's *Masonry Dissected* 1730	*The Bolt-Coleraine MS.*, *1728* (From the Bristol Transcript *op.cit.*)
Tunc unus ex Senioribus teneat Librum, ut illi vel ille ponant vel ponat Manus supra Librum: tum Praecepta debeant legi.	Tunc Unus Ex Senioribus teneat Librum ut illi vel illem ponant vel ponat manus supra Librum Tum praecepta debeant Legi.

Because of the destruction of the 1728 copy of the *Bolt-Coleraine MS.*, in 1941, Bro. Poole was unable to vouch for the accuracy of the Bristol transcript, which was the basis of his reproduction in 1951, and this may perhaps explain the minute differences that appear in the two versions under discussion. But there is another explanation that may be far more satisfying.

All the manuscript versions of the *Old Charges* that can be proved to have been accessible to Prichard in 1730 were in some way connected with the Grand Lodge itself, or with Lord Coleraine, Grand Master in 1727/8. The *Spencer MS.* 1726, the *Songhurst* and *Fisher MSS.*, c.1726, were all copied by William Reid, who was Grand Secretary from 1727-1733. The *Woodford MS.*, (a copy of the *Cooke MS.*, of c.1410) was copied by him in 1728, and it contains an inscription headed 'Ld Coleraine—Gr^d Master'. The *Bolt-Coleraine MS.*, was also copied in 1728, by order of Lord Coleraine, or for his ultimate use.

At this period, two years before Prichard's *Masonry Dissected* was condemned by the Grand Lodge, Prichard obviously had access to the *1728 copy* of the *Old Charges* which eventually became known as the *Bolt-Coleraine MS.*; but in that case, *it is highly probable that he also had access to the original text* from which that copy was made, and that his three clues were extracted from that version which is now lost. All this suggests that Prichard was in touch with William Reid, the Grand Secretary, and perhaps with Lord Coleraine as well.

Immediately following the Latin instruction, Prichard printed a very adequate English translation (*which was not in the Bolt-Coleraine MS.*) and this shows that he had, at the very least, a useful working knowledge of Latin.

The results of this somewhat involved examination of the sources of Prichard's clues show him to have been a man of some education, a student of the early documents of the Craft, with access to one or more texts of the *Old Charges* which were in the custody of the Grand Lodge, or of some of its senior officers; and this implies that in the years preceding the publication of *Masonry Dissected*, he had been a respectable member of a regular Lodge.

We shall see, moreover, when we examine the text of Prichard's three degrees, that he must have had a useful working knowledge of the ritual and usages of that time. Anderson recorded the destruction, in 1720, of 'several very valuable Manuscripts . . . concerning the Fraternity, their Lodges, . . . Secrets and Usages' and we have no means of knowing if Prichard had had access to those or to similar documents. But when we observe how vastly superior his work was to any of the early documents that have survived, and how much of his work can be directly linked with the earlier texts, it is obvious that he was much more than an average student of the Craft, its ritual and procedures.

ACCEPTED MASONRY: pp. 6-7.

Prichard continued his introductory remarks with a note on the Accepted Masonry of his own day:

> . . . Accepted Masonry (as it now is) has not been heard of till within these few Years; no Constituted Lodges or Quarterly Communications were heard of till 1691, when Lords and Dukes, Lawyers and Shopkeepers, and other inferior Tradesmen, Porters not excepted, were admitted into this Mystery or no Mystery;

It would have been difficult for Prichard to give a precise date for the rise of 'Accepted Masonry', but there are records of the 'Accepcon' in the London Masons Company from 1621 onwards, and Plot, in his *Natural History of Staffordshire*, had written in

1686 that 'persons of the most eminent quality . . . did not disdain to be of this *Fellowship*', and that he had found it 'spread more or less all over the Nation'.

Prichard's date, 1691, for the beginning of Quarterly Communications, would be beyond proof nowadays; there is no evidence to support the existence of any such established organization in 1691.

Prichard's division of the classes of men who were joining the Craft, reflected the social distinctions of his own era:

> the first sort [Lords and Dukes] being introduc'd at a very great Expence, the second sort [Lawyers and Shopkeepers] at a moderate Rate, and the latter [inferior Tradesmen, Porters not excepted] for the Expence of six or seven Shillings, for which they receive that Badge of Honour, which (as they term it) is more ancient and more honourable than is the Star and Garter, which Antiquity is accounted, according to the Rules of Masonry, as delivered by their Tradition, ever since *Adam*, which I shall leave the candid Reader to determine.

This appears to be the earliest comparison of the Apron with the 'Star and Garter', in words which have survived some 250 years as part of the Masonic ritual in English Lodges all over the world. This note on the Apron as a Badge of Honour is particularly interesting because there is no mention of the Apron in the text of Prichard's exposure, showing—on his own admission—that his text is incomplete.

The reference to 'their Tradition, ever since *Adam*' is a gentle jibe at the opening words of the historical section of Anderson's first *Book of Constitutions*, 1723:

> *Adam*, our first Parent, ... must have had the Liberal Sciences, particularly *Geometry*, written on his Heart; . . .

Prichard's introductory chapter continued with brief references to some of the mock-Masonic societies of the 1730s, and the final paragraph consisted of a complaint that a Brother, having to withdraw from the Craft because of the 'Quarterly Expenses' would be

> denied the Privilege (as a Visiting Brother) of knowing the Mystery for which he has already paid, which is a manifest Contradiction according to the Institution of Masonry itself . . . .

The tone of this passage seems to suggest that Prichard was perhaps writing about himself as a sufferer under this rule. He cited another example of 'loss of visiting privileges' in the *'Vindication'*, which formed the final chapter of his book.

THE AUTHOR'S VINDICATION OF HIMSELF ... pp. [30], 31;

The contents of this brief section are not at all in keeping with its pompous but promising title, *The Author's Vindication of himself from the prejudiced Part of Mankind'*. By way of vindication, the only reason he could find, to justify him in the breach of his Masonic oath, was that the Obligation had already been published:

> ... the grand Article, *viz.*, the *Obligation*, has several Times been printed in the publick Papers, but is entirely genuine in the *Daily Journal* of *Saturday, Aug. 22.* 1730. which agrees in its Veracity with that deliver'd in this Pamphlet; and consequently when the Obligation of Secrecy is abrogated, the aforesaid Secret becomes of no Effect, and must be quite extinct;

It had indeed been published under the title *'The Mystery of Freemasonry'*, in the *Daily Journal* of 15 August, 1730 (and in several broadsides under various titles); but even if all these had been correct in every particular, their appearance in print could not have released or absolved him of his own oath. (Incidentally, the text in the *Daily Journal* was vastly inferior to Prichard's version).

At this point, and with total irrelevance to his supposed vindication of himself, Prichard entered on a new theme, telling the story of some Masons[6] who

> made a Visitation from the first and oldest constituted Lodge (... in *London*) to a noted Lodge in this City, and was denied Admittance, because their old Lodge was removed to another House, which, ... requires another Constitution, at no less Expence than two Guineas, with an elegant Entertainment, under the Denomination of being put to charitable Uses. ...

He expressed serious doubts as to whether these costs would really be applied to the charitable uses for which such funds were intended, believing that they would 'be expended towards the forming another System of Masonry, the old Fabrick being so ruinous,

---

[6] He described them as 'Operative Masons (but according to the polite Way of Expression, Accepted Masons)'.

...' There is no record of this incident in the Grand Lodge Minutes; and there was no rule in the 1723 *Book of Constitutions* that would have justified a fee for a new Constitution in this case, unless the Brethren who were 'denied Admittance' had actually withdrawn or separated themselves from their original Lodge, in which case Reg. VIII would have applied.

The story, if it were true, might well have influenced Prichard's views on the Masonry of his day and, doubtless, he recounted it as an additional excuse for his defection. His comments on the 'ruinous' condition of the 'Fabrick' of Masonry seem to reflect the resistance to change which must have been generated fairly widely during that era of major changes in the government of the Craft, while the young Grand Lodge was beginning to acquire control over old and new Lodges in London and the Provinces.

In the *Records of the Lodge of Antiquity No. 2* (Original No. 1) pp. 35/6, our late Bro. W. H. Rylands identified the 'first and oldest constituted Lodge ... in London' as a reference to Original No. 1 and examining Prichard's tirade, he came to the conclusion that

> the whole attack is directed not against Masonry in general, but against the new Fashions which threatened the "old Fabrick".

The final paragraph of Prichard's '*Vindication*' claimed that he was induced to publish his exposure 'at the Request of several Masons' and he expressed the hope that it would

> give entire Satisfaction, and have its desired Effect in preventing so many credulous Persons being drawn into so pernicious a Society.

Whether he was actually persuaded, *by Masons*, to undertake the publication is open to doubt and need not be taken seriously. The sting in the *Vindication* is contained in his opening and closing words:

> Of all the Impositions that have appear'd amongst Mankind, none are so ridiculous as the Mystery of Masonry . . . . so pernicious a Society.

These are the only passages in the whole book that are tinged with real animosity. They suggest that the exposure was not published merely as a protest against changes or innovations. Something had embittered him against the Craft and that is the final detail in the portrait of Prichard that we have tried to reconstruct from the evidence that he left for us. He had been a member of a regular Lodge, had read Anderson's *Book of Constitutions* and was a student of the history of the Craft. He was probably well known to senior officers of the Grand Lodge and certainly had free access to documents in which they were deeply interested. Soon after the *Bolt-Coleraine MS.* had been copied, in 1728, an incident had occurred—trivial or serious, we do not know—but it turned him against the Craft, and he betrayed his Obligation.

MASONIC CATECHISMS AND EXPOSURES[7]

Until the late 1600s the only evidence we have on Masonic ritual consists of several versions of the masons' Obligation (in the *Old Charges*) with occasional notes describing how it was administered (as in the Latin instruction quoted on p. 10, above). The earliest versions are simple oaths of fidelity to the King, the trade, and the Master, without any reference to esoteric matters, or penalties. Some of the later versions contain references to secrets, but without details. *The Harleian MS., No. 2054*, c.1650, contains a form of the Masons' obligation which speaks of 'sev'all [i.e. several] words & signs of a free Mason', plural, implying secret modes of recognition for more than one degree, and indicating that the ceremonies were beginning to take on their modern shape, i.e. an obligation and 'entrusting'; but the text gives no other details. From 1598 onwards, there are Scottish Lodge minutes which prove the existence of two degrees, the first for the Entered Apprentice, and the second for the 'Master or Fellow-craft', but they give no information as to the contents of those ceremonies.

Today, there are altogether seventeen Masonic documents that comprise the whole of the surviving evidence on the ritual up to

---

[7] For students of the evolution of Masonic ritual, the following works are particularly recommended: "Masonic Ritual and Secrets before 1717" by the Rev. Herbert Poole, *AQC* 37, pp. 4-43; *The Early Masonic Catechisms*, by Knoop, Jones and Hamer, which contains transcripts of all the texts up to c. 1740, with a valuable Introduction (2nd edn., publ. by the Q.C. Lodge); "An Examination of the Early Masonic Catechisms", by H. Carr, in *AQC* Vols. 83, 84 and 85, in which the contents of the earlier texts are compared with *Masonry Dissected*; *The Genesis of Freemasonry*, pp. 204-293, by Douglas Knoop and G. P. Jones. A less detailed sketch, covering developments up to c. 1813, "600 Years of Craft Ritual", by H. Carr, in *AQC* Vol. 81, may also prove useful.

1730. Seven of these were printed in newspapers, or as broadsides or pamphlets, and all seven were published from motives of curiosity, profit, or spite; hence their general classification as 'Exposures'.

The remaining ten documents are manuscripts, mainly in the form of Question and Answer, occasionally with the addition of notes on various Masonic matters. At least three of these texts (discovered respectively in 1904, 1930 and 1954) were undoubtedly copied out carefully by hand in order to serve as *aides-mémoires* to the ceremonies and they are particularly valuable on that account. All these hand-written texts were obviously prepared for personal use and they are usually described under the more respectable heading of 'Catechisms'.

The senior Grand Lodges (England, Ireland and Scotland) have never issued any official Rituals or Monitors, so that there are no authoritative documents that would provide a proper starting-point for studies on the evolution and development of early Masonic ritual. It is this total absence of officially authorized material that has invested the Catechisms and Exposures with a degree of importance far beyond the interest they would otherwise have merited. Because all such documents—whether hand-written or printed—were compiled in violation of the Mason's oath, they were collectively deemed to be of dubious origin and therefore suspect; and no matter how interesting their contents might be, they were considered unworthy of serious study. In effect, *the more they revealed, the less they were to be trusted, unless it could be proved that the rituals and procedures which they described were linked in some way with the actual Lodge practice of their time.* That kind of proof was not easy to come by, but it did come—in stages —during a period of some thirty years. The story may seem irrelevant here, but it is not possible to make a fair assessment of Prichard's work without knowing how the cloud of mistrust that rested on all such documents was finally removed. It begins with a fragment of ritual, dated 1702, on the opening page of an old Scottish minute book.

THE 'HAUGHFOOT FRAGMENT'

In 1702, a little group of gentlemen, all Masons, decided to found a Lodge in the village of Haughfoot, some twenty miles S.E. of

Edinburgh. Two of them, Sir John Hoppringle of that Ilk and his younger brother, Sir James Pringle, were notable landowners in that district. Another founder, Andrew Thomson, probably a lawyer, was due to become their 'Boxmaster' and he served in that office, i.e. as Treasurer, combining it with the duties of Secretary. He was ordered to buy a minute-book, for which he was reimbursed in due course 'ffourteen shillings Scotts'.

The minute book survives to this day as one of the treasures of the ancient Lodge of Selkirk, No. 18, S.C. Its contents begin, in the middle of a sentence, at the top of page 11, the preceding ten pages having been lost or destroyed. As far as we can reconstruct the story, it seems that Thomson began his records with details of the preliminaries before the foundation of the Lodge, and then continued with what must have been a complete copy, or a précis, of the two-degree ritual of that time. When this was finished, he had filled the first ten pages, and the last five lines of ritual were at the top of page 11, leaving three-quarters of the page blank. But his native Scottish thrift would not allow him to waste that page and, immediately after the end of his ritual text, he added a heading:

'The same day'

and continued with the minutes of the meeting held on 22 December 1702, apparently the first 'working' meeting at which six 'Intrants . . . were duely and orderly admitted apprentice and ffellow Craft'.

The minutes were beautifully kept throughout the next sixty-one years, but the Lodge disappeared in 1763, probably being swallowed up by some of its more powerful neighbours. At some stage in its history—we do not know when—the minute-book must have fallen into the hands of a zealous busy-body, who was so horrified at finding the ritual copied out into its opening pages that he tore out the first ten. He was constrained to leave the last fragment of ritual on page 11 intact, doubtless because that page contained the earliest minutes of the lodge. Hence, the 'Haughfoot fragment', just twenty-nine words of ritual-procedure, preserved since 1702 in the minute-book of a small but very respectable Lodge. They begin in the middle of a sentence:

> of Entrie as the apprentice did Leaving out (The Common Judge.)

> Then they whisper the word as befor—and the master mason grips his hand after the ordinary way.

The 'fragment' with its uninformative references to a whispered word, and a grip given by the 'master mason' did not attract serious attention from scholars because the main body of the text was missing and the surviving words, the 'fragment' could not be matched to any other known text. It was left, so-to-speak, in mid-air, simply because there were no means of ascertaining its real significance.

STAGES IN THE EVALUATION OF THE CATECHISMS AND EXPOSURES

The first hesitant step towards a proper evaluation of the Catechisms and Exposures was taken in 1904, when Bro. W. J. Hughan, a notable scholar and founder of the Q.C. Lodge, compiled a brief note (in *A.Q.C.* Vol. 17, pp. 91/2) on a newly-discovered manuscript that he had just acquired for the Grand Lodge of Ireland. It is now known as The *Chetwode Crawley MS.*, c.1700, and is reproduced in *E.M.C.*, 2nd edn., pp. 35-38. The text is headed

THE GRAND SECRET OR THE FORME OF GIVING THE
MASON-WORD

and it describes, in narrative form, the ritual and procedure of the two admission ceremonies of its day. Its contents are of high importance in our present study and they may be summarized briefly, as follows:

> FOR THE ENTERED-APPRENTICE. The candidate was put 'upon his knees: And after a great many Ceremonies, to frighten him', he took up the Bible and repeated the Oath. He was then 'removed out of the Company with the youngest Mason;' There, he endured further horseplay. Then, still outside the Lodge, he was taught 'the manner of making Guard, which is the Sign, Word & Postures of his Entry'.
> He returned to the Lodge, made the [E.A.] Sign, recited the 'Words of Entry' and made the Sign again. Then, the 'word' was passed by 'the youngest mason' in a whisper to his neighbour who passed it on similarly, and so on all round the Lodge, until it came to the Master, who whispered it to the candidate. (There is a note indicating that the E.A. had *two* Pillar-words). After this there was a Catechism of sixteen Questions and Answers, and that was all.

FOR THE 'MASTER-MASON OR FELLOW-CRAFT. All Apprentices were removed 'non Suffered to stay, but only Mason Masters' and there was no horseplay. The candidate had the same 'Oath administered . . . anew'. He was taken out by 'the youngest Master to learn the words & Signs of ffellowship'. Returning, he gave 'the Master-Sign' (not described) and 'the Same words *of Entry as the prentice did, only leaving out the Common Judge*', i.e. those three words, which *were* in the E.A. greeting. Then '*the Masons whisper the word . . . as formerly*', i.e., the 'word' was passed by the youngest Master in a 'rotational whisper', until it reached the Master. The candidate placed himself in a posture, for what was subsequently described as 'ffive . . . . Points of ffellow-ship', and he gave a whispered greeting to the Brethren. '*Then the Master Mason gives him the word & grips his hand*, and afterwards, all the Masons, which is all to be done to make a perfect Mason'. Associated with this ceremony was a Catechism of only four test Questions and Answers, and that was all for the 'Master-Mason or ffellow-Craft'.

In his notes on '*The Chetwode Crawley MS.*, Bro. Hughan, after having compared it with all the early Exposures and Catechisms that were known in his day, observed that 'the Common Gudge' [*sic*] had been cited as part of the equipment of 'a just and perfect Lodge' in two printed Exposures, *A Mason's Examination*, 1723, and *The Mystery of Free-Masonry*, 1730. To his credit, he was the first to notice the close similarity between the 'Haughfoot fragment' and the comparable section of the *Chetwode-Crawley MS.* (i.e. the words shown in italics in the above summary) but for reasons unknown, probably excessive caution, he dated the newly-found text as 'about the year 1730, or slightly earlier'. Nevertheless, he accorded it a substantial degree of respectability when he wrote that the distinctive features in *Chetwode-Crawley*

> suggest to my mind that it represents a more or less accurate account of the Ceremonies of the period, written by a brother, who took this plan to assist his memory, and who himself had been Admitted as an "Apprentice and Master Mason, or ffellow-Craft" accordingly.

This was a bold admission in 1904, but it was clear that Bro. Hughan's caution, in dating the text c.1730, had misled him as to the true significance of the obvious relationship between the 'Haughfoot fragment' and the *Chetwode Crawley MS.*

In 1924, Bro. Herbert Poole, in his "Masonic Ritual and Secrets before 1717" (*AQC.* 37 p. 7) discussed the same question and concluded that

> ... the latter [i.e. the *Chetwode-Crawley MS.*] though it may have been *copied* as late as 1730, must be regarded as a faithful description of a ceremony which was worked at the very beginning of the eighteenth century.

This was proper recognition at last, not merely of the *C.C.MS.* for itself, but of the authentication which it gained from the 'fragment' of ritual in the minute book of the Haughfoot Lodge.

Bro. Poole's conclusions were completely justified in 1930 on the discovery of a sister text to the *C.C.MS.*, now known as the *Edinburgh Register House MS.*, (because it was found in the Public Record Office of Edinburgh.) It bore an endorsement "Some Questiones Anent the mason word 1696" and that date 1696, after strict examination, is accepted by the experts. The two texts differ in many respects, e.g., in spelling, phrasing, and in the 'catechism-narrative' sequence of the Edinburgh text, which is the reverse of that in the *C.C.MS.* In spite of these minor differences, there is no doubt that they are descended from a common original, and they certainly describe the same two ceremonies.

In 1954, a third version was discovered, now known as the *Kevan MS.*, *c.*1714, and this—because of the omission of several words and phrases—is clearly a defective text. Yet, there is no doubt that all three describe the same general procedure. Their differences, indeed, are helpful, because it is obvious that *they were not copied from each other*, implying—so long as they can be *authenticated*—that they represent lodge working over a fairly wide area in the south of Scotland. The authentication comes from the 'Haughfoot fragment' which is clearly a précis of the corresponding passages in all three texts.

One major benefit that arises from these documents, as soon as they are recognized as respectable versions of the ritual of their day, is that *they provide, collectively, a firm basis for further studies and for testing the validity of some of the later texts*; but it must be emphasized that the three sister-texts, now often described as the 'Edinburgh group', represent only Scottish practice.

The English Masonic ceremonies, so far as may be judged from surviving evidence, were largely based on the *Old Charges* or *MS.*

Constitutions. In their early form they consisted of an invocation or opening prayer; a reading of some part of the 'history' of the Craft; a recital of the 'Charges' or regulations; an obligation of fidelity, taken 'upon the book' (as indicated in several versions of the 'Latin instruction' quoted on p. 10 above). Originally that was all; but in the 17th century, when we find versions of the *Old Charges* that contain references to 'secrets', and to several 'words & signs' etc., it is obvious that the ceremonies had been expanded to include some form of 'entrusting'. At this stage, the English ceremonies were already beginning to resemble the Scottish forms.

It would not be practicable, here, to make a prolonged study of how the practices of the two countries became merged. Gradually, the ritualistic influence of the *Old Charges* or *MS. Constitutions* declined; but there is no doubt that

> ... both types of operative ceremony, the one depicted in the *MS. Constitutions*, and the one depicted in the *MS. Catechisms*, have undoubtedly contributed to the development of present-day working, and justify us in saying that the existing working has not a single, but a twofold origin.[8]

It is only necessary to stress that so far as the Catechisms and Exposures are concerned, the best of the English texts (when they begin to appear from c.1700 onwards) are in harmony with their Scottish counterparts. Generally, they complement each other, and often, a document, in one group, furnishes details that are lacking in the other. In this way, the sixteen texts that preceded Prichard's work supply a valuable body of evidence to show the sources of much of the material in *Masonry Dissected*.

MASONRY DISSECTED—THE TEXT OF THE EXPOSURE

There is a peculiar fascination attaching to the study of the text of Prichard's exposure, not only because it was the first publication that claimed to describe a system of three degrees, but also because of the variety of the problems that are involved. The work, as a whole, was unlike any of the earlier documents of its kind, both in its general structure and in the manner in which its parts are

---

[8] *The Genesis of Freemasonry*, by Knoop and Jones, M'ter. Univ. Press, 1947 p. 217. This major work is unfortunately out of print and rarely to be found except in Masonic libraries.

presented. Much of Prichard's material was already in existence, but some very important sections had never appeared in manuscript or in print; yet, there is good reason to believe that he did not invent those novelties, but had simply collected and arranged them.

In their Introduction to the *Early Masonic Catechisms* (pp. 11-13 and 18-19) the authors, discussing the early documents up to c.1740, were able to find textual affinities that might have formed a basis for classifying them in four separate groups, with Prichard's *Masonry Dissected* as the first of a fifth grouping; but this left them with six highly individualistic texts which did not bear 'a close affinity to any other known document' and they were forced to conclude that 'there is not sufficient material available to formulate a satisfactory classification'. There is nevertheless, good reason to believe that these groups represent *separate streams* of ritual.

Masonry Dissected, no matter how well it deserved to be placed at the head of a separate group, might well have been included with the six that could not be classified. It was not only the longest and most comprehensive document of its kind, but it also contained items that were more-or-less closely connected with most of the earlier texts. This suggests that it did not necessarily represent the working of a particular lodge, but may have been a composite of several different workings, a distinct possibility, since there was no official control of the ritual or procedures.

Generally, Prichard produced his text for each of the three degrees in the form of a catechism, or a 'Question and Answer Lecture', which took place, presumably, *after* a candidate had passed that particular degree, i.e., the catechism was not a ceremony in itself, but an exercise in the explanation and interpretation of the ritual and procedure relevant to a particular degree.

There were certainly some omissions. Prichard made no mention of a 'Prayer', or of any kind of 'Charge to a newly admitted Brother': it may be that these were not customary in Prichard's Lodges. But his ritual text also omitted all reference to the Apron, though he mentioned the 'Badge of Honour' on page (7) and actually quoted some of the words which accompanied the investiture. These are minor blemishes, however, and they do not seriously detract from the interest or the value of the work as a whole.

The Questions in Prichard's catechism fall readily into three groups:

1. Test questions which were doubtless used prior to the admission of an unknown visitor to a lodge, but which were also designed for test purposes, outside, or away from, the lodge.
2. Questions relating to the actual ceremonies and depicting the preparation of the candidates, and floorwork or procedure inside the lodge.
3. Questions relating to Lodges and Masonry generally, e.g., the 'Form of the Lodge', its jewels, lights, furniture, the composition of a Lodge, the situation and duties of its officers, principles, modes of recognition etc., etc. This group also included much new material of an explanatory or mildly symbolical nature.

The new explanatory material marked an important stage in the expansion of the catechisms. *The Edinburgh Register House MS.*, 1696, contained brief narrative descriptions of the E.A. and F.C. ceremonies, but it had only fifteen Questions and Answers for the E.A., and two for the 'Master or Fellow-craft'. From c.1700 onwards, most of the documents of this class, both in manuscript and print, showed the introduction of materials that had not appeared in the earlier texts. They may have represented separate streams of ritual, or the practice of particular localities; but by 1730, we find much of this material—from several sources—in *Masonry Dissected*. Prichard had ninety-two Q. & A. for the E.A., thirty-two for the F.C., and thirty for the '*Master's* Degree'. A typical example of this expansion is a question in the *Sloane MS., 3329, c.*1700:

Q. wch is the mast^{ers} place in the Lodge

It appeared in various forms in most of the texts that followed, and by the time it was printed in *Masonry Dissected*, it had grown into eight questions, beginning 'Where stands your Master?', with answers covering all the officers down to the 'Junior Enter'd 'Prentice', their situations, jewels and duties.

It would not be practicable here to undertake an examination of Prichard's sources for all his material.[9] The authenticity or trustworthiness of his work can best be checked by comparison with earlier documents of the same class. Virtually the whole of his *Enter'd 'Prentice's* Degree can be traced back (as in the *Sloane*

---
[9] A detailed study of this aspect of Prichard's material will be found in *A.Q.C.* 83, pp. 337-357; *AQC.* 84, pp. 293-307 and *AQC* 85, pp. 331-348.

example just quoted) to texts from 1696 onwards and the same applies to substantial parts of his F.C. and M.M. degrees. But when we find major items in Prichard's text for which there are no precedents, we can only test their reliability by seeing how much of that material was accepted and used in the best of the publications that appeared in the following decades. These aspects of Prichard's work will be discussed in the Notes that follow the Facsimile. For the present we are concerned with one section of his work that distinguished *Masonry Dissected* from all its predecessors, i.e., the Hiramic Legend.

THE FIRST HIRAMIC LEGEND—SOURCES

From Q. 133 to the end of the catechism, the text gives us the earliest known version of the 'Hiramic Legend' and (apart from one interesting procedural note to Q. 149) it is all in the form of question and answer. Our study, at this stage, is only concerned with Prichard's sources.

The story of Hiram's part in the building of Solomon's Temple is told twice in the Old Testament (1. Kings VII and 11 Chron. II). Masonic sources for the Legend are almost non-existent. The *Old Charges*, in their historical section, trace the 'science' of building through a collection of early Biblical characters in which Solomon and his Temple are barely mentioned, and Hiram appears usually under a pseudonym, Aynon, Aymon, etc., in numerous variations. But there is no mention of Hiram's death in the Biblical accounts, nor in the commentaries, nor in any of the *Old Charges*. Indeed, nowhere in all of these early sources is there any trace of the various incidents which made up the story, now generally known as the Hiramic Legend, and it seems certain that Prichard's version—the earliest that has come down to us—was a comparatively late introduction into Craft working.

If we examine his text to ascertain its principal elements, the story divides into four main sections:

1. The Master-mason of K.S.T. who refused to divulge the M.M. Word, and was slain in consequence, i.e., 'faithful unto death'.
2. The assassins hide the body and bury it.
3. Solomon orders the search and *the searchers agree amongst*

themselves that 'if they do not find the Word in him or about him, the first Word should be the Master's Word'
4. The discovery of the corpse. The 'raising' on the F.P.O.F. and the 'Funeral'.

In all these items there is only one 'constant' that had appeared in practically all the earlier Masonic catechisms and exposures, i.e. the 'Points of Fellowship'. Sixteen of these texts have survived that preceded the publication of *Masonry Dissected*, many of them differing widely from each other. Yet, in spite of their differences, fourteen of them, from 1696 onwards, contain descriptions of the 'Points of Fellowship' and some five or six of them furnish their own sadly-debased versions of the word that is supposed to have accompanied those Points.

There can be no doubt whatever that this part of the 'Hiramic Legend' was very strongly established in Craft usage long before Prichard's work appeared, yet in all these there is no hint of a *Hiramic* Legend, except in one late version, *The Wilkinson MS.*, c.1727, which contains a curious answer to one of its questions, without mention of the 'Points of Fellowship':

Q. What is the form of your Lodge
A. An Oblong Square
Q. Why so
A. The Manner of our Great Master Hiram's grave

This tiny fragment of evidence proves nothing of any importance, but it does at least imply that 'Hiram's grave' was of some interest to the Craft at that time.

So, we are left, in the period 1696 to 1730, with the 'Points of Fellowship' and a Word, parts of the skeleton of a legend, and it is very difficult to believe that this is all there was. Throughout the middle ages and well into the 18th century, hundreds of years before the invention of radio and television, stories and legends, music and songs were the main social recreation of the people. Indeed, the *Old Charges* themselves, with their numerous legends concerning the supposed founders of the Craft, and others 'who loved masons well and gave them their charges', suggest very strongly that there must have been a store of craftlore, *not necessarily in the ritual*, with which the masons entertained themselves off duty. As to the 'Points of Fellowship', even at the stage when the ritual contained no hint of a legend, it is impossible to believe that any group of masons could have recited the words, or demonstrated the postures that they described, without some kind of story or legend in explanation of their origin, or meaning.

In our search for sources, there is one document of supreme importance, the *Graham MS*, 1726, which must be cited frequently in connexion with other aspects of Prichard's work. That text is unique in many respects. It is headed:

> THE WHOLE INSTITUTIONS OF FREE MASONRY
> OPENED AND PROVED BY THE BEST OF TRADITION
> AND STILL SOME REFERANCE TO SCRIPTURE

Its compiler was probably a churchman, or at least a deeply religious Christian, and he exercised his powers of interpretation on the catechism and on many aspects of the ritual that have rarely been handled in that way. After he had finished with the catechism, which consisted largely of selected questions that lent themselves to his purpose, he completed his manuscript with a collection of legends, each of them with a kind of Masonic twist in its tail. The characters were mainly Biblical and one of the legends concerns three brothers who went to their father's grave

> ... for to try if they could find anything about him ffor to Lead them to the vertuable secret which this famieous preacher had ... Now these 3 men had allready agreed that if they did not ffind the very thing it self that the first thing that they found was to be to them as a secret they not Douting but did most ffirmly be Lieve that God was able and would ... cause what they did find for to prove as vertuable to them as if they had received the secret at ffirst from God himself .... so came to the Grave finding nothing save the dead body all most consumed away takeing a greip at a ffinger it came away so from Joynt to Joynt so to the wrest [wrist] so to the Elbow so they R Reared up the dead body and suported it setting ffoot to ffoot knee to knee Breast to breast Cheeck to cheeck and hand to back and cryed out help o ffather ... so one said here is yet marow in this bone ...
>
> (*E.M.C.* pp. 92/3)

It is hardly necessary to comment on the resemblances between this extract and the relevant portions of Prichard's 'Master's Part', but it is noteworthy that here too, the searchers *agreed in advance* 'that if they did not ffind the very thing it self the first thing that they found was to be to them as a secret'. The details of decay, which led to what Prichard called 'the Slip', are very similar in both texts, though the 'greips' in the *Graham MS.* do not agree with those in Prichard's '*NB* note' to Q.149.

The major difference between the two versions is in the principal characters. In Prichard, the victim was Hiram, the builder; in the 1726 version it was Father Noah and it was his three sons, Shem, Ham and Japhet, who 'Reared him up' by the 'Points of Fellowship'.

We have already had occasion to refer to separate 'streams' of ritual; the *Graham MS,* with its Noah Legend, provides us with a 'separate stream' of legend, and we need not be surprised to find that the earliest story of a raising *within a Masonic context*, concerned Noah instead of Hiram. The *Graham MS.* may have emanated from Yorkshire, and if we were fortunate enough to find similar documents from Kent or Cornwall we might expect to find the same legend, with still different characters.

The *Graham MS.* contains another collection of legends, one of which seems (to the present writer at least) to have considerable bearing on our search. It concerns another architect in the Old Testament who achieved great fame by his works. At last, being near to death,

> . . . he disired to be buried in the valey of Jehosephate and have cutte over him according to his diserveing [i.e. an appropriate epitaph on his tombstone] which was performed . . . . . and this was cutte as follows—
> Here Lys the flowr of masonry superiour
> of many other companion to a king and
> to two princes a brother
> Here Lys the heart all secrets could conceall
> Here lys the tongue that never did reveal—
> now after his death the inhabitance there about did think that the secrets of masonry had been totally Lost . . . .
> (*E.M.C.*pp. 93/4)

Had this been an epitaph for H.A. it could not have been more apt, especially 'the tongue that never did reveal'; but the hero, in this case, was Bezaleel, architect of the Tabernacle and designer of the Temple equipment and furnishings. The relationship of this legend to the 'faithful unto death' theme in Prichard's Hiramic legend is neither so clear nor so close as in the Noah legend; yet its very existence is sufficient to show that such legends were current in craft-lore, ready to be adapted and embodied in the ritual by those who were interested in expanding it for Speculative use.

There is good reason to believe that the compiler of the *Graham MS.* was not the inventor of the legends. In his catechism he only provided *the religious interpretation of traditional materials*, and that was almost certainly the case in his Noah legend. The date of his manuscript, 1726, is no real guide to the age of the Noah and Bezaleel stories. If Hiram the builder had been the principal character in those stories, we would be unable to date them much earlier than Prichard's Hiramic legend, which may be assumed to represent practice in the London area. The fact that the *Graham* legends deal with different characters and exhibit other textual differences as well, shows that they represent 'separate streams' of legend, and that implies a greater antiquity and a more widespread usage.

One more document, a newspaper advertisement dated 1726, may be cited here as evidence that many items in Prichard's work, including several phrases relevant to the Hiramic Legend, were well known to Masons some years before *Masonry Dissected* was published. It was found in a collection of newspaper-cuttings in the Grand Lodge Library. The name of the journal is unknown, but internal evidence in the text confirms the date, 1726. The advertisement is headed 'Antediluvian Masonry'.

The whole piece is a jibe against Dr. John Theophilus Desaguliers, who was Grand Master in 1719, for innovations he is supposed to have introduced into the Craft, and it was apparently written by someone well informed on contemporary ritual and practice. The following brief extracts are selected only because of their relevance in the study of Prichard's Hiramic Legend:

> ... There will likewise be a Lecture giving a particular Description of the Temple of Solomon ... with the whole History of the Widow's Son killed by the Blow of a Beetle, afterwards found three Foot East, three Foot West, and three Foot perpendicular, and the necessity there is for a Master to well understand the Rule of Three.

Later, there are references, *inter alia*, to

> ... oblong-Squares, cassia, and mossy Graves ...

and the piece is signed

> By Order of the Fraternity
> Lewis Giblin, M.B.N.
> (*A.Q.C.*23, pp.325-6)

Returning now to the emergence of the Hiramic Legend, we have proof of the existence of the two-degree system from 1598 onwards. In 1696, we have proof of the 'Points of Fellowship' together with the 'Word' as the core of the second degree in that system, and there is reasonable probability that they may have been there in 1598 if not earlier. Jointly, those 'Points' with the 'Word' were the prime elements among the materials which subsequently became the legend of the third degree. Until *Masonry Dissected* was published in 1730, one or both of those elements had appeared in most of the earlier ritual documents, English as well as Scottish, always without explanation. Yet, the curious details of the 'Points' and the nature of the 'Word' that accompanied them, compel us to accept that there must have been a legend of some sort, within the Craft-lore of those days, that would explain their origin and meaning. Indeed, to those who witnessed them, the actual movements in the 'Points' must have been—in themselves—a useful reminder of the legend from which they were derived.

The absence of documentary proof, makes it impossible to determine when the legend or its elements first came into Craft usage. But when we consider the 1590s as a possible date for the 'Points' and 'Word', the variety of detail in the Noah and Bezaleel legends in the *Graham MS.*, 1726, with the scarcely veiled hints in the 'Antediluvian' advertisement of that year, and 'the Manner of our Great Master Hiram's grave' in the *Wilkinson MS.*, of c.1727, it is obvious that *the source materials of the legend were much earlier than 1696*, though we have no proof of them *in the ritual* until the 1720s.

THE EVOLUTION OF THE THREE-DEGREE SYSTEM

The evolution of the trigradal system is one of the major unsolved problems of Masonic research. We know a great deal about the third degree, but we do not know why it came into practice, when or where it began, or who was responsible for its evolution. No less important is the question 'How did it take root and spread as it did, at a time when there was no governing body that organized the contents and dissemination of the ritual, and no prescribed working of any kind?'

The reason for our ignorance on these matters is the absence of records of the third degree or the trigradal system in the *Books of Constitutions* and Grand Lodge minutes of that period. In the 1723 *B. of C.*, at a time when there were only two degrees in practice, Regulation XIII had prescribed that

> Apprentices must be admitted Masters and Fellow-Craft only here, unless by a Dispensation.

'Only here', i.e. in the Grand Lodge; this was an attempt, on the part of the Grand Lodge, to arrogate to itself the right to confer the senior degree. Dr. Anderson, the compiler-editor of the regulations, was a Scotsman and he used the joint title 'Master and Fellow-craft' in exactly the same way as it had been used in the 'Edinburgh-group' of catechisms (and in early Scottish Lodge minutes from 1598 onwards) to describe the second degree in the two-degree system.

The reasons for this Regulation may have originated in a desire for close control and good management of the Lodges, but the rule was an infringement of their inherent rights, which must have been deeply resented and which proved wholly unworkable. On 27 November 1725, this part of the Regulation was repealed:

> A Motion being made that Such part of the 13th Article of the Gen[ll] Regulations relating to the Making of Ma[rs] only at a Quarterly Communication, may be repealed, And that the Ma[rs] of Each Lodge with the Consent of his Wardens, And the Majority of the Brethren being Ma[rs] may make Ma[rs] at their Discretion
> Agreed Nem. Con. (*Q.C.A.*, X, p.64).

At face value this minute might be taken to mean that the Grand Lodge was giving permission for Lodges to confer the third degree, but it is equally likely that this was simply intended to give back to the Lodges their ancient right to confer the second degree of 'Master and Fellow-Craft'.

There is some reason to believe that Reg. XIII and the resentment it aroused was the reason for the splitting of the first degree into two parts, thus creating an 'artificial' second degree (which was already known in its essentials to all Entered Apprentices) and thereby making the original second degree into the third. This certainly describes what was happening, but it is impossible to say definitely whether the Grand Lodge minute of 27 November 1725 referred to the second degree of the two-degree system, or the third in the newly-evolving trigradal system. The only official evidence on the subject appears in Charge IV in the 1723 *Book of Constitutions*, relating to the qualifications of Wardens, and in the altered version of the same Charge in the second edition in 1738:

> In 1723: No Brother can be a *WARDEN* until he has pass'd the part of a *Fellow-Craft*; ...
> In 1738: The *Wardens* are chosen from among the *Master-Masons*, ...

Grand Lodge had obviously recognized the status of Master-Masons, but there is certainly *no trace of the third degree being promulgated by the Grand Lodge, or that any of its leading members were engaged in framing this new arrangement.* As a result, we are compelled to seek even the faintest hints wherever they are to be found.

The earliest evidence suggesting the evolution of a three-degree system is in the *Trinity College, Dublin, MS.*, 1711. It begins as a very short catechism of only eleven Q. and A., followed by a paragraph in narrative form, which lists a collection of signs, words, etc. In the course of this section, various modes of recognition are allocated to the Enterprentice, fellow craftsman, and Master (i.e. M.M.) the latter having the world's worst description of the Points of Fellowship, with a word that is quite unbelievably debased. This text, despite its numerous defects, lists the three separate grades with distinguishing modes of recognition belonging to each, the first hint that someone was experimenting with the idea of a system of three degrees. (*E.M.C.*, p. 70)

The "Mason's Examination", 1723, was the first exposure to be printed in a London newspaper *The Flying Post or Post-Master*, 11-13 April 1723. Its catechism had been substantially expanded and it contained no hint of trigradal practice; but the text contains a rhymed verse which appears to allocate certain distinguishing characteristics to three grades, 'enter'd Mason, Fellow, and Master-

Mason'. The details do not agree with those in the *Trinity College, Dublin, MS.*, and some of them are puzzling, but they are, nevertheless, a possible hint of a system of three degrees. (ibid, pp. 71-2)

However interesting such hints may be, they cannot be accepted as *proof* of the trigradal system in practice. For that *proof* we must have actual Lodge minutes recording the conferment of the third degree, minutes which were scarce in 1720-1740, and very few have survived to this day. We do have a minute describing the conferment of the third degree in May 1725 in London and that is the earliest surviving record; but that ceremony took place in a Musical Society, *not in a Lodge*, and it was Masonically highly irregular. But the story is interesting, and well documented.

In December 1724, there was a London Lodge which met at the Queen's Head Tavern, Hollis Street, in the Strand, only a few hundred yards from the present Grand Lodge building. It is recorded in the Grand Lodge Minute book, in the 'List of Regular Constituted Lodges . . . ' dated 27 November 1725, with a list of fourteen of its members, though there were probably several more whose names are not listed. The membership was small and select, and there were among them several cultured gentlemen who were keenly interested in music and architecture. Around the end of 1724, seven of the members with one Brother from another Lodge decided to 'fix and establish a Mutual Society of True Lovers of Music and Architecture', which was duly founded on 18 February 1725, under the title '*Philo Musicae et Architecturae Societas Apollini*'.

They drew up a book of 'Constitutions and Orders' (a masterpiece of the art of calligraphy, now in the British Museum) which displayed on its title-page the armorial bearings of the Founders, good evidence of their social status! These men enjoyed their Masonry and among their Rules was one which prescribed:

> 'That no person shall be admitted as a
> Visitor unless he be a Free Mason'

and that rule applied, of course, to the members of the Society.

The preamble to their 'Constitutions' listed the names of their Founders, with details of when and where they were made Masons. They also kept similar records for the Masons who joined their Society. Among these details there is a note that 'some time before'

1 February 1725 four of the Founders of the Musical Society 'were regularly Pass'd Masters in the before mentioned Lodge of Hollis Street'.

This may well refer to a third degree but, because we have no record of the two earlier degrees being conferred on these Brethren, we must accept the possibility that this note may be a reference only to the second degree in the two-degree system.

For indisputable evidence of the three degrees being conferred on one candidate, there are two entries in the same preamble followed by an item in the minutes of the Musical Society, and they are summarized here:

> Preamble: 22 December 1724. At a meeting attended by the Grand Master, His Grace the Duke of Richmond, who acted as Master on that evening, 'Charles Cotton Esqr was made a Mason by the said Grand Master'.
>
> Preamble: 18 February 1725. 'And before We Founded This Society A Lodge was held Consisting of Masters Sufficient for that Purpose In Order to Pass Charles Cotton Esqr Mr Papillon Ball and Mr Thomas Marshall Fellow Crafts. . . .' [Note: 'A lodge was held' and *because that happened on the day the Society was founded*, it is not certain whether the Lodge was a regular meeting of the Hollis Street Lodge, or only a meeting of members of the Musical Society. But this was certainly the second degree for Bros. Cotton and Ball, the latter having been initiated in the Lodge on 1 February 1725.]

> *Philo-Musicae* Minutes: 12 May 1725. 'Our Beloved Brothers & Directors of this Right Worshipfull Societye whose Names are here. Underwritten (viz)
> Brother Charles Cotton Esq^e
> Broth^r Papillon Ball
> Were regularly passed Masters . . .
>   (*Q.C.A.*, IX, p.41)

There can be no doubt that Cotton and Ball had received the three degrees, though the third was highly irregular, having been conferred at a meeting of the Musical Society, not a Lodge.

On 20 May 1725 the Grand Lodge minutes record

> That there be a L$\overline{re}$ [Letter] wrote to the foll^g Brethren to desire them to attend the Grand Lodge at the next Quarterly

> Communication (vizt) [seven names of the principal Founders and officers of the Philo-Musicae.]

The letter was apparently ignored, but the Musical Society had visits from the Junior Grand Warden on 2 September 1725 and the Senior Grand Warden on 23 December 1725 and the Society disappeared early in 1727.

The earliest unimpeachable record of the third degree is in the minutes of Lodge Dumbarton Kilwinning, now No. 18 (Scotland). At its foundation meeting on 29 January 1726 there were present the W.M. with seven M.M's., six F.C's., and three E.A.'s. At the next meeting on 25 March 1726:

> Gabrael Porterfield who appeared in the January meeting as a Fellow Craft was unanimously admitted and received a Master of the Fraternity and renewed his oath and gave in his entry money.

Porterfield was a Fellow Craft at the foundation meeting of the new Lodge. At the next meeting, he was 'received a Master of the Fraternity and renewed his oath', i.e. another ceremony; and he 'gave in his entry money', i.e. he paid for it. There can be no doubt that this was the third degree.

In December 1728, Lodge Greenock Kilwinning at its foundation meeting prescribed *separate fees* for being 'entered as Apprentices . . . passed Fellow-Craft . . . and . . . when raised Master Mason'.

The adoption of the three-degree system was very slow. The earliest record of a third degree in the Lodge of Antiquity, then No. 1., was in 1737. From c.1733 onwards, there are records of Masters' Lodges usually attached to regular Lodges, but meeting generally on Sundays, for conferring the third degree; but these Masters' Lodges were few in number and ephemeral in character and most of them disappeared within two or three years. No details of their rituals have survived.

An interesting example of the slow adoption of the new system appears in the minutes of the ancient Lodge of Kelso, No. 58 (Scotland) whose minutes begin in 1701. On 18 January 1754, three visiting Brethren from the Lodge Canongate from Leith, were invited to act as Master and Wardens in order to demonstrate how Fellow crafts were passed in and around Edinburgh, and two candidates were duly passed by the visiting team.

After the Lodge was closed, the Brethren continued conversing about 'the forms and Practice of this Lodge in particular', when

> ..... a most essential defect of our Constitution was discovered, viz—that this Lodge had attained only to the two Degrees of Apprentices and Fellow Crafts, and know nothing of the Master's part, whereas all Regular Lodges over the World are composed of at least the three Regular Degrees of Master, Fellow Craft, and Prentice .....

Here, at Kelso, almost thirty years after the trigradal system had begun to come into use, the members of the Lodge had never heard of it! They re-opened the Lodge and the three visitors, with three other Master Masons who were present, conducted the M.M. degree and raised five Brethren that same evening. (W.F. Vernon. *Hist. of Freemasonry in Roxburghshire & Selkirkshire, p. 120*)

Reverting now to 1730, in the *Mystery of Free-Masonry*, which was published only two months before Prichard's work appeared, the same slow development is emphasized in two notes following a catch question!

> Q. How old are you? A. Under 5, or under 7, which you will.
>
> N.B. When you are first made a Mason, you are only entered Apprentice; and till you are made a Master, or, as they call it, pass'd the Master's Part, you are only an enter'd Apprentice, and consequently must answer under 7; for if you say above, they will expect the Master's Word and Signs.
>
> Note, There is not one Mason in an Hundred that will be at the Expence to pass the Master's Part, except it be for Interest. (*E.M.C.* p. 155)

The general contents of this exposure, and of the N.B. note quoted here, suggest very strongly that the anonymous author was referring only to the second degree in the two-degree system when he spoke of the slow adoption of the Master's Part; but the same comment would have applied, even more forcefully, to the Master's Part in the newly evolving trigradal system.

The point to be emphasized is that 'The Master's Degree' in Prichard's work was still in a very early stage of development.

There was no uniformity of practice in the Lodges and no official control of ritual. Most of the Lodges in 1730 would still have been working the earlier system of two degrees and no more; and many of them, especially in the Provinces, had never heard of the third degree. Others, mainly in and around London, were using the new trigradal system at whatever stage of development they had acquired it.

Our study inevitably suggests that the change from two to three degrees was almost certainly the work of Speculative Masons who took the opportunity of extending the moral, religious and philosophical aspects of the Craft by the use of allegory, legend and explanatory materials which brought new life and spirit into the ritual. Thus the 'Letter G' and the 'Middle Chamber' came into the second degree and the Hiramic legend came into the third. That does not imply that these ritual novelties were new inventions; it is *far more likely that they were traditional materials in Craft-lore*, long before the Speculative expansion had begun.

The obvious question arises, 'How, in the absence of official instructions and encouragement, was this great change achieved?' The answer seems to be that no major innovation was involved. The contents of the three-degree system were, in all essentials, the same materials that had existed in the original two, but now in a new arrangement and enhanced by the addition of illustrations and legends which had probably existed long before the changes were contemplated. The actual spread of the new system would have been achieved by plain 'contagion'. One Lodge would make a supposed improvement in its working, and if it proved popular, their work would be copied by those neighbouring Lodges that were able to witness it; and they in turn adopted, arranged and added new materials as they saw fit. Nobody was accused of innovation!

When and where did it begin? It is impossible to answer these questions with any degree of certainty. The evidence of the *Trinity College, Dublin MS.*, quoted above, would suggest Ireland in 1711; but the date seems too early and there is no supporting evidence in lodge minutes, or in contemporary ritual texts. The Mason's Examination, 1723, plus the Philo Musicae evidence in 1725, would seem to be more reliable as to date and location, London, with the probability that the latter group were practising a ceremony that they had acquired in the lodge to which most of them belonged, at the Queen's Head Tavern in Hollis Street, London. The indisputable evidence from Dumbarton Kilwinning, in 1726, would seem to be a much stronger claim, but whether the three-degree system actually began there is rather doubtful. Scotland had no Grand Lodge until 1736 and they do not appear to have had the outstanding Speculative members who might have introduced the changes. In England, George Payne, who was Grand Master in 1718, and Dr. J. T. Desaguliers, G.M. in 1719, were the enthusiastic and devoted leaders who might well have been responsible, and there were others, e.g. Martin Folkes and Francis Drake, who might have helped at a later stage.

Why did it happen? Under conditions of operative masonry practising the two-degree system, there was only one degree for 'Master and Fellow-craft': *inside* the Lodge those two classes were equal, both fully trained masons. But *outside* the Lodge, the Master (i.e. M.M.) was entitled to operate as an employer, while the F.C. was only an employee. Inevitably the time would come when there had to be a separate degree for each grade, but under the operative system changes were rare and they usually happened only in response to changing conditions in the mason trade.

In *c*.1725 operative masonry was almost at its last gasp. The strict controls formerly exercised by the operative (territorial) Lodges had virtually disappeared and most of the Lodges, both in England and Scotland, were of mixed operative and non-operative membership, with no influence whatever in trade control. The reasons for needing an extra degree had apparently disappeared, but the desire probably remained, and the new conditions were favourable to change.

Another possible reason has already been noted, i.e. the desire of the English Masons to evade the restrictions implicit in Reg. XIII of the *B. of C.* which would have limited the Lodges to conferring only the Apprentice degree.

Perhaps the most satisfying explanation is that the changes reflect the earliest results of Speculative influence on the Craft after it had been organized under a Grand Lodge. So long as the cultured elements in the Craft were enjoying their Freemasonry, this kind of expansion was inevitable. It is possible that Reg. XIII may have encouraged their efforts, but the establishment of the Grand Lodge was itself the strongest stimulus.

'Masonry Dissected'—Its Influence on the Ritual

It is fitting that the final chapter of this study of Prichard's work should be devoted—however briefly—to a survey of its influence on the Craft ritual. There is no doubt that the book enjoyed a phenomenal success, both immediate and long-term, and all the major historians of the ritual are agreed that *Masonry Dissected* was largely responsible for the stabilization of the English ritual in its formative years under the first Grand Lodge.

The reason for this success is obvious. In 1730, at a time when Freemasonry was growing in popularity and when Speculative influence was beginning to make itself felt, *there was still a total absence of printed versions of officially-approved ritual*. *Masonry Dissected*, regardless of the private reasons that had prompted its publication, provided an accessible, soundly-based, and reasonably accurate working, which would enable the Lodges to achieve some kind of standard, incomparably superior to any that had appeared in all the earlier texts, whether in manuscript or print.

After the three pamphlet editions in October 1730, and the pirated newspaper versions in the same month, there were at least nineteen further editions up to 1760, when the next series of English exposures began to appear. There were, indeed, four or five rival exposures published during those thirty years, all of them worthless catchpennies. Indeed, there are simply *no records of new developments* in English ritual during the thirty-year gap, from 1730 to 1760 and throughout that period Prichard's work held the field.

It was translated into French by an anonymous writer, who published it in 1738 under the title *La Réception Mystérieuse* after having added his own comments, with a reprint of the *Réception d'un Frey-Maçon*, the first of the French exposures, originally published in 1737. All these parts were joined together as the first chapter of a book which also contained several chapters on European history etc., of no Masonic interest. Surprisingly, the title-page gave Samuel Prichard's name as the sole author. The compiler was not a Freemason and that explains a number of curious and often amusing errors in translation. It was also translated into German and Dutch in 1738 (*E.F.E.* pp. 9-39).

When the best of the French exposures began to appear in the 1740s we begin to see some of the long-term effects of Prichard's work. *L'Ordre des Francs-Maçons Trahi* (the *Trahi*) was first published in 1745, fifteen years after *Masonry Dissected*, and it serves as an excellent illustration of what was happening. Its catechism, now substantially expanded by many new items that had come into French practice during the intervening years, was still basically Prichard's work. In fact, two questions and answers out of every three in the *Trahi* were directly taken from *Masonry Dissected*, either word-for-word, or with French embellishments; and the translation was far better than that in *La Réception Mystérieuse*. The Hiramic legend, which had first appeared in *Masonry Dissected* in the course of answers to a dozen or so questions, was now the subject of a long narrative recital, and the *Trahi* also contained a valuable description of the floorwork and procedures of the ceremony. But when those new materials are stripped away, the basis is still Prichard's work.

The *Trahi* achieved no fewer than seventeen editions in French, up to 1781. It also appeared in German in 1745 under the title *Der Verrathene Orden der Freimaurer*, with three more German impressions in that year and three further editions in 1758, 1763 and 1778. The influence of all these French and German editions on European ritual must have been incalculable.

In England, after the thirty-year gap, the new streams of exposures began to appear in 1760 and 1762 representing both Moderns' and Antients' practices; their catechisms still contained a great deal of Prichard's work, though so much new material had come into use that the original nucleus becomes less obvious. A certain amount of French influence had also remained and it is interesting to read the *English* descriptions of the procedure of the third degree, punctuated by a couple of paragraphs describing the corresponding procedure in the French Lodges.

Many more expansions and changes were to take place before the English ritual was standardized in 1813, but those are strictly beyond the scope of our present study. Nevertheless, the student who will take the trouble to compare his modern ritual with that of Prichard in 1730 will often be astonished to see how much has survived.

HARRY CARR

London
February, 1975

FACSIMILE PAGES

of

SAMUEL PRICHARD'S

Masonry Dissected

For ease of reference, the Questions in Prichard's catechism have been numbered in our reproduction of the text, and in the Notes that follow it. They were not numbered in the original publications in 1730.

MASONRY
Dissected:

BEING

A Universal and Genuine

DESCRIPTION

OF

All its B R A N C H E S from the Original to this Present Time.

As it is deliver'd in the

Constituted Regular Lodges

Both in CITY and COUNTRY,

According to the

Several Degrees of ADMISSION.

Giving an Impartial ACCOUNT of their Regular Proceeding in Initiating their New Members in the whole Three Degrees of MASONRY.

VIZ.

I. ENTER'D 'PRENTICE, } { II. FELLOW CRAFT.
{ III. MASTER.

To which is added,

The Author's VINDICATION of himself.

By SAMUEL PRICHARD, *late Member of a*
CONSTITUTED LODGE.

LONDON:

Printed for J. WILFORD, at the *Three Flower-de Luces* behind the *Chapter house* near St. Paul's. 1730. (Price 6 d)

Samuel Prichard maketh Oath, That the Copy hereunto annexed is a True and Genuine Copy in every Particular.

Jur' 13. *Die Oct.*
1730. *coram me*,
R. Hopkins.

Sam. Prichard.

TO THE

R^t. Worſhipful and Honourable

FRATERNITY

OF

Free and Accepted Maſons.

Brethren and Fellows,

IF the following Sheets, done without Partiality, gains the univerſal Applauſe of ſo worthy a Society, I doubt not but its general Character will be diffuſed and eſteemed among the remaining Polite Part of Mankind: Which,

DEDICATION.

Which, I hope, will give intire Satisfaction to all Lovers of Truth, and I shall remain, with all humble Submission, the Fraternity's

Most Obedient

Humble Servant,

SAM. PRICHARD

Masonry Dissected.

THE original Inftitution of Mafonry confifteth on the Foundation of the Liberal Arts and Sciences; but more efpecially on the Fifth, *viz.* **Geometry.** For at the Building of the Tower of *Babel*, the Art and Myftery of Mafonry was firft introduc'd, and from thence handed down by *Euclid*, a worthy and excellent Mathematician of the *Egyptians*, and he communicated it to *Hiram*, the Mafter-Mafon concern'd in the Building of *Solomon*'s Temple in *Jerufalem*, where was an excellent and curious Mafon that was the chief under their Grand-Mafter *Hiram*, whofe Name was *Mannon Grecus*, who taught the Art of Mafonry to one *Carolos Marcil* in *France*, who was afterwards elected King of *France*, and from thence was brought into *England* in the Time of King *Athelftone*, who order'd an Affembly to be held once every Year at *York*, which was

was the first Introduction of it into *England,* and Masons were made in the Manner following.

Tunc unus ex Senioribus teneat Librum, ut illi vel ille ponant vel ponat Manus supra Librum ; tum Præcepta debeant legi. i. e. *Whilst one of the Seniors holdeth the Book, that he or they put their Hands upon the Book, whilst the Master ought to read the Laws or Charges.*

Which Charges were, That they should be true to one another without Exception, and should be obliged to relieve their Brothers and Fellows Necessities, or put them to labour and reward them accordingly.

But in these latter Days Masonry is not composed of Artificers, as it was in its primæval State, when some few Catechetical Questions were necessary to declare a Man sufficiently qualified for an Operative Mason.

The Terms of Free and Accepted Masonry (as it now is) has not been heard of till within these few Years; no Constituted Lodges or Quarterly Communications were heard of till 1691, when Lords and Dukes, Lawyers and Shopkeepers, and other inferior Tradesmen, Porters not excepted,

cepted, were admitted into this Myftery or no Myftery; the firft fort being introduc'd at a very great Expence, the second fort at a moderate Rate, and the latter for the Expence of fix or seven Shillings, for which they receive that Badge of Honour, which (as they term it) is more ancient and more honourable than is the Star and Garter, which Antiquity is accounted, according to the Rules of Mafonry, as delivered by their Tradition, ever fince *Adam*, which I shall leave the candid Reader to determine.

From the Accepted Mafons fprang the Real Mafons, from both fprang the *Gormogons*, whofe Grand-Mafter the *Volgi* deduces his Original from the *Chinefe*, whofe Writings, if to be credited, maintains the *Hypothefes* of the *Pre-Adamites*, and confequently muft be more antique than Mafonry.

The moft free and open Society is that of the *Grand Kaihebar*, which confifts of a felect Company of Refponfible People, whofe chief Difcourfe is concerning Trade and Bufinefs, and promoting mutual Friendfhip without Compulfion or Reftriction.

But if after the Admiffion into the Secrets of Mafonry, any new Brother fhould
diflike

(8)

dislike their Proceedings, and reflect upon himself for being so easily cajoled out of his Money, declines the Fraternity or secludes himself upon the Account of the Quarterly Expences of the Lodge and Quarterly Communications, notwithstanding he has been legally admitted into a Constituted and Regular Lodge, shall be denied the Privilege (as a Visiting Brother) of knowing the Mystery for which he has already paid, which is a manifest Contradiction according to the Institution of Masonry itself, as will evidently appear by the following Treatise.

Enter'd

Enter'd

Enter'd 'Prentice's DEGREE.

[1] Q. FROM whence came you?
A. From the Holy Lodge of St. *John*'s.

[2] Q. What Recommendations brought you from thence?
A. The Recommendations which I brought from the Right Worſhipful Brothers and Fellows of the Right Worſhipful and Holy Lodge of St. *John*'s, from whence I came, and Greet you thrice heartily well.

[3] Q. What do you come here to do?
A. Not to do my own proper Will,
But to ſubdue my Paſſion ſtill;
The Rules of Maſonry in hand to take,
And daily Progreſs therein make.

[4] Q. Are you a Maſon?
A. I am ſo taken and Accepted to be amongſt Brothers and Fellows.

[5] Q. How ſhall I know that you are a Maſon?
A. By Signs and Tokens and perfect Points of my Entrance.

[6] Q. What are Signs?
A. All Squares, Angles and Perpendiculars.

[7] Q. What are Tokens?
A. Certain Regular and Brotherly Gripes.

[8] Exam. Give me the Points of your Entrance.
Resp. Give me the first, and I'll give you the second.

[9] Exam. I Hail it.
Resp. I Conceal it.

[10] Exam. What do you Conceal?
Resp. All Secrets and Secresy of Masons and Masonry, unless to a True and Lawful Brother after due Examination, or in a just and worshipful Lodge of Brothers and Fellows well met.

[11] Q. Where was you made a Mason?
A. In a Just and Perfect Lodge.

[12] Q. What makes a Just and Perfect Lodge?
A. Seven or more.

[13] Q. What do they consist on?
A. One Master, two Wardens, two Fellow-Crafts and two Enter'd 'Prentices.

[14] Q. What makes a Lodge?
A. Five.

[15] Q. What do they consist of?
A. One Master, two Wardens, one Fellow-Craft, one Enter'd 'Prentice.

[16] Q. Who brought you to the Lodge?
A. An Enter'd 'Prentice.

[17] Q. How did he bring you?
A. Neither naked nor cloathed, bare-foot nor shod, deprived of all Metal and in a right moving Posture.

[18] Q. How got you Admittance?
A. By three great Knocks.

[19] Q. Who receiv'd you?
A. A

A. A Junior Warden.

[20] Q. How did he dispose of you?

A. He carried me up to the North-East Part of the Lodge, and brought me back again to the West and deliver'd me to the Senior Warden.

[21] Q. What did the Senior Warden do with you?

A. He presented me, and shew'd me how to walk up (by three Steps) to the Master.

[22] Q. What did the Master do with you?

A. He made me a Mason.

[23] Q. How did he make you a Mason?

A. With my bare-bended Knee and Body within the Square, the Compass extended to my naked Left Breast, my naked Right Hand on the Holy Bible; there I took the Obligation (or Oath) of a Mason.

[24] Q. Can you repeat that Obligation.

A. I'll do my Endeavour. (*Which is as follows.*)

I Hereby solemnly Vow and Swear in the Presence of Almighty God and this Right Worshipful Assembly, that I will Hail and Conceal, and never Reveal the Secrets or Secresy of Masons or Masonry, that shall be Revealed unto me; unless to a True and Lawful Brother, after due Examination, or in a Just and Worshipful Lodge of Brothers and Fellows well met.

I furthermore Promise and Vow, that I will not Write them, Print them, Mark them, Carve them or Engrave them, or cause them to be Written, Printed, Marked, Carved or Engraved on Wood

B 2 *or*

or Stone, so as the *Visible Character or Impression of a Letter may appear, whereby it may be unlawfully obtain'd.*

All this under no less Penalty than to have my Throat cut, my Tongue taken from the Roof of my Mouth, my Heart pluck'd from under my Left Breast, them to be buried in the Sands of the Sea, the Length of a Cable-rope from Shore, where the Tide ebbs and flows twice in 24 Hours, my Body to be burnt to Ashes, my Ashes to be scatter'd upon the Face of the Earth, so that there shall be no more Remembrance of me among Masons.

So help me God.

[25] Q. What Form is the Lodge?
A. A long Square.

[26] Q. How long?
A. From East to West.

[27] Q. How broad?
A. From North to South.

[28] Q. How high?
A. Inches, Feet and Yards innumerable, as high as the Heavens.

[29] Q. How deep?
A. To the Centre of the Earth.

[30] Q. Where does the Lodge stand?
A. Upon Holy Ground, or the highest Hill or lowest Vale, or in the Vale of *Jehosaphat*, or any other secret Place.

[31] Q. How is it situated?
A. Due East and West.

Q. Why

[32] Q. Why so?
A. Because all Churches and Chappels are or ought to be so.

[33] Q. What supports a Lodge?
A. Three great Pillars.

[34] Q. What are they called?
A. Wisdom, Strength and Beauty.

[35] Q. Why so?
A. Wisdom to contrive, Strength to support, and Beauty to adorn.

[36] Q. What Covering have you to the Lodge?
A. A clouded Canopy of divers Colours (or the Clouds.)

[37] Q. Have you any Furniture in your Lodge?
A. Yes.

[38] Q. What is it?
A. *Mosaick* Pavement, Blazing Star and Indented Tarsel.

[39] Q. What are they?
A. *Mosaick* Pavement, the Ground Floor of the Lodge, Blazing Star the Centre, and Indented Tarsel the Border round about it.

[40] Q. What is the other Furniture of a Lodge?
A. Bible, Compass and Square.

[41] Q. Who do they properly belong to?
A. Bible to God, Compass to the Master, and Square to the Fellow-Craft.

[42] Q. Have you any Jewels in the Lodge?
A. Yes.

[43] Q. How many?
A. Six. Three Moveable, and three Immoveable.   Q. What

| 44 | Q. What are the Moveable Jewels?
A. Square, Level and Plumb-Rule.
| 45 | Q. What are their Uses.
A. Square to lay down True and Right Lines, Level to try all Horizontals, and the Plumb-Rule to try all Uprights.
| 46 | Q. What are the Immoveable Jewels?
A. Trasel Board, Rough Ashler, and Broach'd Thurnel.
| 47 | Q. What are their Uses?
A. Trasel Board for the Master to draw his Designs upon, Rough Ashler for the Fellow-Craft to try their Jewels upon, and the Broach'd Thurnel for the Enter'd 'Prentice to learn to work upon.
| 48 | Q. Have you any Lights in your Lodge?
A. Yes, Three.
| 49 | Q. What do they represent?
A. Sun, Moon and Master-Mason.
>N.B. *These Lights are three large Candles placed on high Candlesticks.*
| 50 | Q. Why so?
A. Sun to rule the Day, Moon the Night, and Master-Mason his Lodge.
| 51 | Q. Have you any fix'd Lights in your Lodge?
A. Yes.
| 52 | Q. How many?
A. Three.
>N.B. *These fix'd Lights are Three Windows, suppos'd (tho' vainly) to be in every Room where a Lodge is held, but more properly*

properly the four Cardinal Points according to the antique Rules of Masonry.

[53] Q. How are they situated?
A. East, South and West.

[54] Q. What are their Uses?
A. To light the Men to, at and from their Work.

[55] Q. Why are there no Lights in the North?
A. Because the Sun darts no Rays from thence.

[56] Q. Where stands your Master?
A. In the East.

[57] Q. Why so?
A. As the Sun rises in the East and opens the Day, so the Master stands in the East [*with his Right Hand upon his Left Breast being a Sign, and the Square about his Neck*] to open the Lodge and to set his Men at Work.

[58] Q. Where stands your Wardens?
A. In the West.

[59] Q. What's their Business?
A. As the Sun sets in the West to close the Day, so the Wardens stand in the West [*with their Right Hands upon their Left Breasts being a Sign, and the Level and Plumb-Rule about their Necks*] to close the Lodge and dismiss the Men from Labour, paying their Wages.

[60] Q. Where stands the Senior Enter'd 'Prentice?
A. In the South.

Q. What

[61] Q. What is his Business?
A. To hear and receive Instructions and welcome strange Brothers.

[62] Q. Where stands the Junior Enter'd 'Prentice?
A. In the North.

[63] Q. What is his Business?
A. To keep off all Cowans and Eves-droppers.

[64] Q. If a Cowan (or Listner) is catch'd, how is he to be punished?
A. To be plac'd under the Eves of the Houses (in rainy Weather) till the Water runs in at his Shoulders and out at his Shoos.

[65] Q. What are the Secrets of a Mason?
A. Signs, Tokens and many Words.

[66] Q. Where do you keep those Secrets?
A. Under my Left Breast.

[67] Q. Have you any Key to those Secrets?
A. Yes.

[68] Q. Where do you keep it?
A. In a Bone Bone Box that neither opens nor shuts but with Ivory Keys.

[69] Q. Does it hang or does it lie?
A. It hangs.

[70] Q. What does it hang by?
A. A Tow-Line 9 Inches or a Span.

[71] Q. What Metal is it of?
A. No manner of Metal at all; but a Tongue of good Report is as good behind a Brother's Back as before his Face.

N. B.

Masonry Dissected. 17

The Key is the Tongue, the Bone Bone Box the Teeth, the Tow-Line the Roof of the Mouth.

[72] Q. How many Principles are there in Masonry?
A. Four.

[73] Q. What are they?
A. Point, Line, Superficies and Solid.

[74] Q. Explain them.
A. Point the Centre (*round which the Master cannot err*) Line Length without Breadth, Superficies Length and Breadth, Solid comprehends the whole.

[75] Q. How many Principle-Signs?
A. Four.

[76] Q. What are they?
A. Gututral, Pectoral, Manual and Pedestal.

[77] Q. Explain them.
A. Guttural the Throat, Pectoral the Breast, Manual the Hand, Pedestal the Feet.

[78] Q. What do you learn by being a Gentleman-Mason.
A. Secrefy, Morality and Goodfellowship.

[79] Q. What do you learn by being an Operative Mason?
A. Hue, Square, Mould-stone, lay a Level and raise a Perpendicular.

[80] Q. Have you seen your Master to-day?
A. Yes.

C   Q. How

[81] Q. How was he Cloathed?
A. In a Yellow Jacket and Blue Pair of Breeches.

N.B. *The Yellow Jacket is the Compasses, and the Blue Breeches the Steel Points.*

[82] Q. How long do you serve your Master?
A. From Monday Morning to Saturday Night.

[83] Q. How do you serve him?
A. With Chalk, Charcoal and Earthen Pan.

[84] Q. What do they denote?
A. Freedom, Fervency and Zeal.

[85] Ex. Give me the Enter'd 'Prentice's Sign.
Resp. Extending the Four Fingers of the Right Hand and drawing of them cross his Throat, is the Sign, and demands a Token.

N.B. *A Token is by joining the Ball of the Thumb of the Right Hand upon the first Knuckle of the Fore-finger of the Brother's Right Hand that demands a Word.*

[86] Q. Give me the Word.
A. I'll letter it with You.

[87] Exam. BOAZ. [N.B. *The Exam. says* B, *Resp.* O, *Exam.* A, *Resp.* Z, *i. e.* Boaz.] Give me another.
Resp. JACHIN. [N.B. Boaz *and* Jachin *were two Pillars in* Solomon's Porch. 1 Kings, chap. vii. ver. 21.]

[88] Q. How old are you?
A. Under Seven. [*Denoting he has not pass'd Master.*]

Q. What's

| 89 | Q. What's the Day for?
A. To See in.
| 90 | Q. What's the Night for?
A. To Hear.
| 91 | Q. How blows the Wind?
A. Due East and West.
| 92 | Q. What's a Clock?
A. High Twelve.

The End of the Enter'd 'Prentice's Part.

Fellow-Craft's Degree.

[93] Q. Are you a Fellow-Craft?
A. I am.
[94] Q. Why was you made a Fellow-Craft?
A. For the sake of the Letter G.
[95] Q. What does that G denote?
A. Geometry, or the fifth Science.
[96] Q. Did you ever travel?
A. Yes, East and West.
[97] Q. Did you ever work?
A. Yes, in the Building of the Temple.
[98] Q. Where did you receive your Wages?
A. In the middle Chamber.
[99] Q. How came you to the middle Chamber?
A. Through the Porch.
[100] Q. When you came through the Porch, what did you see?
A. Two great Pillars.
[101] Q. What are they called?
A. J. B. *i.e. Jachim* and *Boaz*.
[102] Q. How high are they?
A. Eighteen Cubits.
[103] Q. How much in Circumference?
A. Twelve Cubits.

} *Vide* 1 *Kings, Chap.* 7.

Q. What

[104] Q. What were they adorn'd with?
A. Two Chapiters.
[105] Q. How high were the Chapiters?
A. Five Cubits.

Vide 1 Kings, Chap. 7.

[106] Q. What were they adorn'd with?
A. Net-Work and Pomegranates.
[107] Q. How came you to the middle Chamber?
A. By a winding Pair of Stairs.
[108] Q. How many?
A. Seven or more.
[109] Q. Why Seven or more?
A. Because Seven or more makes a Just and Perfect Lodge.
[110] Q. When you came to the Door of the middle Chamber, who did you see?
A. A Warden.
[111] Q. What did he demand of you?
A. Three Things.
[112] Q. What were they?
A. Sign, Token, and a Word.
> N.B. *The Sign is placing the Right Hand on the Left Breast, the Token is by joining your Right Hand to the Person that demands it, and squeezing him with the Ball of your Thumb on the first Knuckle of the middle Finger, and the Word is* Jachin.

[113] Q. How high was the Door of the middle Chamber?
A. So high that a Cowan could not reach to stick a Pin in.

[114] Q. When you came into the middle, what did you see?
A. The Resemblance of the Letter G.

[115] Q. Who doth that G denote?
A. One that's greater than you.

[116] Q. Who's greater than I, that am a Free and Accepted Mason, the Master of a Lodge.
A. The Grand Architect and Contriver of the Universe, or He that was taken up to the top of the Pinnacle of the Holy Temple.

[117] Q. Can you repeat the Letter G?
A. I'll do my Endeavour.

The Repeating of the Letter G.

Resp. In the midst of *Solomon*'s Temple there stands a G,
A Letter fair for all to read and see,
But few there be that understands
What means that Letter G.

[118] Ex. My Friend, if you pretend to be
Of this Fraternity,
You can forthwith and rightly tell
What means that Letter G.

Resp. By Sciences are brought to Light
Bodies of various Kinds,
Which do appear to perfect Sight;
But none but Males shall know my Mind.

[119] Ex. The Right shall.
Resp. If Worshipful.

Ex. Both

[120] Ex. Both Right and Worshipful I am,
To Hail you I have Command,
That you do forthwith let me know,
As I you may understand.
Resp. By Letters Four and Science Five
This G aright doth stand,
In a due Art and Proportion,
You have your Answer, Friend.
N.B. *Four Letters are* Boaz.
Fifth Science Geometry.

[121] Ex. My Friend, you answer well,
If Right and Free Principles you discover,
I'll change your Name from Friend,
And henceforth call you Brother.
Resp. The Sciences are well compos'd
Of noble Structure's Verse,
A Point, a Line, and an Outside;
But a Solid is the last.

[122] Ex. God's good Greeting be to this our happy Meeting.
Resp. And all the Right Worshipful Brothers and Fellows.

[123] Ex. Of the Right Worshipful and Holy Lodge of St. *John*'s.
Resp. From whence I came.

[124] Ex. Greet you, greet you, greet you thrice, heartily well, craving your Name.

[125] Resp. *Timothy Ridicule.*
Exam. Welcome, Brother, by the Grace of God.

N.B.

N. B. *The Reason why they Denominate themselves of the Holy Lodge of St. John's, is, because he was the Fore-runner of our Saviour, and laid the first Parallel Line to the Gospel (others do assert, that our Saviour himself was accepted a Free-Mason whilst he was in the Flesh) but how ridiculous and prophane it seems, I leave to judicious Readers to consider.*

The End of the Fellow-Craft Part.

The Master's DEGREE.

[126] Q. ARE you a Master-Mason?
A. I am; try me, prove me, disprove me if you can.

[127] Q. Where was you pass'd Master?
A. In a Perfect Lodge of Masters.

[128] Q. What makes a Perfect Lodge of Masters?
A. Three.

[129] Q. How came you to be pass'd Master?
A. By the Help of God, the Square and my own Industry.

[130] Q. How was you pass'd Master?
A. From the Square to the Compass.

[131] Ex. An Enter'd 'Prentice I presume you have been.
R. *Jachin* and *Boaz* I have seen;
A Master-Mason I was made most rare,
With Diamond, Ashler and the Square.

[132] Ex. If a Master-Mason you would be,
You must rightly understand the Rule of Three.
And * M. B. shall make you free: * Machbenah
And what you want in Masonry,
Shall in this Lodge be shewn to thee.

D   R. Good

R. Good Masonry I understand;
The Keys of all Lodges are all at my Command.

[133] Ex. You're an heroick Fellow; from whence came you?

R. From the East.

[134] Ex. Where are you a going?

R. To the West.

[135] Ex. What are you a going to do there?

R. To seek for that which was lost and is now found.

[136] Ex. What was that which was lost and is now found?

R. The Master-Mason's Word.

[137] Ex. How was it lost?

R. By Three Great Knocks, or the Death of our Master *Hiram*.

[138] Ex. How came he by his Death?

R. In the Building of *Solomon*'s Temple he was Master-Mason, and at high 12 at Noon, when the Men was gone to refresh themselves, as was his usual Custom, he came to survey the Works, and when he was enter'd into the Temple, there were Three Ruffians, suppos'd to be Three Fellow-Crafts, planted themselves at the Three Entrances of the Temple, and when he came out, one demanded the Master's Word of him, and he reply'd he did not receive it in such a manner, but Time and a little Patience would bring him to it: He, not satisfied with that Answer, gave him a Blow, which made him reel; he went to the other Gate, where being accosted in the same manner,

and

and making the same Reply, he received a greater Blow, and at the third his *Quietus*.

[139] Ex. What did the Ruffians kill him with?
R. A Setting Maul, Setting Tool and Setting Beadle.

[140] Ex. How did they dispose of him?
R. Carried him out at the West Door of the Temple, and hid him under some Rubbish till High 12 again.

[141] Ex. What Time was that?
R. High 12 at Night, whilst the Men were at Rest.

[142] Ex. How did they dispose of him afterwards?
R. They carried him up to the Brow of the Hill, where they made a decent Grave and buried him.

[143] Ex. When was he miss'd?
R. The same Day.

[144] Ex. When was he found?
R. Fifteen Days afterwards.

[145] Ex. Who found him?
R. Fifteen Loving Brothers, by Order of King *Solomon*, went out of the West Door of the Temple, and divided themselves from Right to Left within Call of each other; and they agreed that if they did not find the Word in him or about him, the first Word should be the Master's Word; one of the Brothers being more weary than the rest, sat down to rest himself, and taking hold of a Shrub, which came easily up, and perceiving the Ground to have been broken, he Hail'd his Brethren,

Brethren, and pursuing their Search found him decently buried in a handsome Grave 6 Foot East, 6 West, and 6 Foot perpendicular, and his Covering was green Moss and Turf, which surprized them; whereupon they replied, *Muscus Domus Dei Gratia*, which, according to Masonry, is, *Thanks be to God, our Master has got a Mossy House*: So they cover'd him closely, and as a farther Ornament placed a Sprig of *Cassia* at the Head of his Grave, and went and acquainted King *Solomon*.

| 146 | Ex. What did King *Solomon* say to all this?

R. He order'd him to be taken up and decently buried, and that 15 Fellow-Crafts with white Gloves and Aprons should attend his Funeral [*which ought amongst Masons to be perform'd to this Day.*]

| 147 | Ex. How was *Hiram* rais'd?

R. As all other Masons are, when they receive the Master's Word.

| 148 | Ex. How is that?

R. By the Five Points of Fellowship.

| 149 | Ex. What are they?

Hand to Hand [1], Foot to Foot [2], Cheek to Cheek [3], Knee to Knee [4], and Hand in Back [5].

> N. B. *When Hiram was taken up, they took him by the Fore-fingers, and the Skin came off, which is called the Slip; the spreading the Right Hand and placing the middle Finger to the Wrist, clasping the Fore-finger and the Fourth to the Sides*
> *of*

of the *Wrist*; is called the *Gripe*, and the Sign is placing the *Thumb* of the *Right Hand* to the *Left Breast*, extending the *Fingers*.

Ex. What's a Master-Mason nam'd.

R. *Cassia* is my Name, and from a Just and **Perfect** Lodge I came.

Ex. Where was *Hiram* inter'd?

R. In the *Sanctum Sanctorum*.

Ex. How was he brought in?

R. At the West-Door of the Temple.

Q. What are the Master-Jewels?

A. The Porch, Dormer and Square Pavement.

Q. Explain them.

A. The Porch the Entring into the *Sanctum Sanctorum*, the Dormer the Windows or Lights within, the Square Pavement the Ground Flooring.

Ex. Give me the Master's Word.

R. Whispers him in the Ear, and supported by the Five Points of Fellowship before-mentioned, says *Machbenah*, which signifies *The Builder is smitten*.

N. B. *If any Working Masons are at Work, and you have a desire to distinguish Accepted Masons from the rest, take a Piece of Stone, and ask him what it smells of, he immediately replies, neither Brass, Iron, nor Steel, but of a Mason; then by asking him, how old he is, he replies above Seven, which denotes he has pass'd Master.*

The End of the Master's Part.

The Author's Vindication of himself from the prejudiced Part of Mankind.

OF all the Impositions that have appear'd amongst Mankind, none are so ridiculous as the Mystery of Masonry, which has amus'd the World, and caused various Constructions and these Pretences of Secrecy, invalid, has (tho' not perfectly) been revealed, and the grand Article, *viz.* the *Obligation,* has several Times been printed in the publick Papers, but is entirely genuine in the *Daily Journal* of *Saturday, Aug.* 22. 1730. which agrees in its Veracity with that deliver'd in this Pamphlet ; and consequently when the Obligation of Secrecy is abrogated, the aforesaid Secret becomes of no Effect, and must be quite extinct ; for some Operative Masons (but according to the polite Way of Expression, Accepted Masons) made a Visitation from the first and oldest constituted Lodge (according to the Lodge Book in *London*) to a noted Lodge in this City, and was denied Admittance, because their old Lodge was removed to another House, which, tho' contradictory to this great Mystery, requires another Constitution, at no less Expence than two Guineas, with an elegant Entertainment, under the Denomination of being put to charitable Uses, which if juftly applied, will give great Encomiums to fo worthy an Undertaking, but it is very much doubted, and moſt reaſonable to think it will be expended towards the forming another Syſtem of Maſonry, the old Fabrick being ſo ruinous, that, unleſs repair'd by ſome occult Myſtery, will ſoon be annihilated.

I was induced to publiſh this mighty Secret for the publick Good, at the Requeſt of ſeveral Maſons, and it will, I hope, give entire Satisfaction, and have its deſired Effect in preventing ſo many credulous Perſons being drawn into ſo pernicious a Society.

F I N I S.

NOTES

It is perhaps necessary to emphasize that in the following Notes on the Questions and Answers in *Masonry Dissected* we are primarily concerned with the sources of Prichard's materials. This is not a study of present-day ritual and it takes no account of the materials that came into Masonic practice, or of those that disappeared, after 1730. During the next hundred years there were, indeed, some massive changes, but the modern student will find little difficulty in recognizing how much has changed and how much has survived since Prichard's day.

ENTER'D 'PRENTICE'S DEGREE

TEST QUESTIONS. Q. 1-10

The first two questions in Prichard's exposure represent the kind of examination that might have been conducted before admitting an unknown visitor, and the answer to Q. 2 is a form of 'greeting' very similar to the version in the *Sloane MS.*, *c*.1700. (Q. 3, with its answer in doggerel rhyme, seems to be a late interpolation; there is no trace of it in the earlier texts).

With only one or two exceptions, all the catechisms begin with, or contain, a set of *test questions*, e.g. Are you a Mason? How shall I know it? etc., with cautious *shared answers* as in Prichard's Q. 8 and Q. 9:

    Q. 8. Exam. Give me the Points of your Entrance
           Resp. Give me the first, and I'll give you the second
    Q. 9. Exam. I Hail it
           Resp. I Conceal it.

The 'Edinburgh group' of texts contain a special answer to be given if non-Masons were present, indicating that these questions were also to be used outside, or away from, the Lodge.

Three of Prichard's opening questions (Q.8,9,10) are headed 'Exam'. and 'Resp'. instead of the usual Q. and A., a curious change, which is not easily explained at this stage. Clearly, there was something unusual about these items, a problem which will be discussed later, when we find several further sets of questions in all three degrees, which are similarly headed.

There seems to have been no rule as to how many of the questions were used for test purposes. Prichard's Q. 1 to 10 seem to have formed a fairly comprehensive set, which may have been shortened or extended according to circumstances.

A JUST AND PERFECT LODGE. Q. 11-15

Q. 11 to 15 deal with the numbers of the several grades of Masons who formed a Lodge. The numbers varied in the different texts, e.g. *The Graham MS.*, 1726, said 'any od number from 3 to 13', but the majority agree with Prichard's seven, or five. The earliest versions usually included a clause specifying the solitary location, while two of the later prints add to the requisite numbers the words 'with Square, Compass, and Common Gudge' i.e. a gauge or templet.

PREPARATION OF THE CANDIDATE. Q. 17

Q.17. How did he bring you [to the Lodge]?

A. Neither naked nor cloathed, bare-foot nor shod, deprived of all Metal and in a right moving Posture.

This is the first Q & A in *M.D.* that gives a hint of some kind of preparation of the candidate in those days. Later, in the preliminaries to the Obligation there is further information on this point:

Q. 23. How did he make you a Mason?

A. With my bare-bended Knee and Body within the Square, the Compass extended to my naked Left Breast, my naked Right Hand on the Holy Bible; there. . . .

Earlier details on the subject of 'preparation' appear in several documents. *The Dumfries No. M.S.*, c.1710, has:

Q. hou were you brought in

A. shamfully w^t a rope about my neck

Q. whay a rop about your neck

A. to hang me If I should Betry may trust

The Graham MS. 1726:

[Q.] How came you into the Lodge

[A.] poor and penyless blind and Ignorant of our secrets

Several later documents which touch on this point are more in accord with Prichard, but it is obvious that there were substantial variations in practice. There are three possible explanations:

(1) Varying systems in use in different parts of the country
(2) Some of the details may be complementary to each other, e.g., the preparation implied in the *Dumfries MS.* might easily be combined with that in the *Graham MS.*
(3) New customs superseding older ones, perhaps as a result of Speculative influence.

PERAMBULATION. Q. 20-21

Questions 20 and 21 describe some sort of perambulation around the Lodge, followed by three steps leading up to the Master. This procedure finds some support in texts of c.1727 to 1730, suggesting that it was then of recent introduction.

THE POSTURE FOR THE OBLIGATION. Q. 23

The three texts of the 'Edinburgh group' agree that the candidate took the Obligation 'upon his knees', i.e., on both knees and most of our texts, from 1696 onwards, indicate a kneeling posture. The *Dumfries No. 4 MS.*, c.1710, mentions the left-knee, and three of the later ones, 1726-1730 mention the 'right-knee'. Three of the late versions, 1724-c.1727, say 'with Square and Compass at my Breast'; three, including *M.D.*, mention only the Compass in that position. *The Grand Mystery Laid Open*, 1726, speaks of 'the Holy Bible at my Breast', but it is a rather frivolous piece, including many gibberish words.

The *Mystery of Free-Masonry*, 1730, has a footnote, '. . . . the Square under the Right-Elbow' and the *Sloane MS.*, c.1700, in a rather complicated passage, seems to imply a Square 'under the right Arme', but it is possible that these are both related to the second degree in a two-degree system.

Prichard's Q. 23 (quoted under 'Preparation of Candidate', above) gives a succinct description of the 'Posture', but there were variations elsewhere.

THE OBLIGATION. Q. 24

The Oath or Obligation was the essential element in the admission ceremony throughout the recorded history of the Craft. In mediaeval times, it was a simple oath of fidelity to the King, the Trade and the Master, and there were no physical penalties. The earliest version of the *Old Charges*, *The Regius MS.*, c.1390, prescribed that

> .... all shall swear the same oath of the masons, be they willing, be they loth.

Early references to secrecy in the *Old Charges* were not yet concerned with modes of recognition, but were designed to protect the *trade secrets* of the Master, or employer. The *Harleian MS. No. 2054*, c.1650, was the earliest text that contained a form of the obligation which prescribed secrecy concerning *several* 'words & signes of a free Mason' (implying more than one degree) and the introduction of secret modes of recognition may help to date the appearance of physical penalties in the Masonic ritual, though they were not yet embodied in the 17th century Obligations that are known to us.

The Obligation in the *Edinburgh Register House MS.*, 1696, contains the injunction

> ... you shall not reveal any pairt of what you shall hear or see at this time whither by word nor write nor put it in wryte at any time nor draw it with the point of a sword, or any other instrument upon the snow or sand. ...

This is the earliest version of the modern 'indite, carve, mark, engrave....' etc. *There is no penalty in the Obligation*, but an E.A. penalty appears, for the first time, in the subsequent 'words of entrie'.

The *Sloane MS.*, c.1700, has a simple Obligation of secrecy, but it includes the familiar words 'without any manner of Equivocation or mentall Resarvation'. There is still no penalty in the Ob., itself; it does appear, however, in the catechism.

The Ob. in the *Dumfries No. 4. MS.*, c.1710, is also very brief and without penalties, but the catechism contains several novelties. In addition to the rope 'to hang me If I should Betry may trust' (mentioned under 'Preparation of Candidate', above) it has:

Q. what punishment is inflicted on these y^t reveals ye secret

A. y^r heart is to be taken out alive y^r head to be cut of & y^r bodys to be buried in ye sea mark & not in any place Qr christians are buried

This is the first hint of multiple penalties.

The 'Mason's Examination' was the earliest *printed* exposure, published in a London newspaper in 1723; it did not contain a form of the Ob., but the narrative description of the ceremony says:

> ... he swears to reveal no Secrets ... on Pain of having his Throat cut. ...

Later, in the catechism, this answer is expanded by an alternative:

> ... of having my Throat cut, or Tongue pull'd out.

From c.1727 onwards, we can date the appearance of the far more elaborate Obligations, which enlarge the precautionary injunctions 'not to write, carve, engrave, etc.,' and also contain *multiple penalties within the text of the Obligations*. It is in this section that we have the best evidence showing how closely Prichard's work was influenced by contemporary sources.

The *Wilkinson MS.*, is dated c.1727, but may be slightly later. In its Obligation, the candidate undertook that he would 'not write them, work them, mark them, Point them or Engrave them ...' and its penalties are very similar to those in Prichard's text. Because the *Wilkinson* is a manuscript, it is unlikely that Prichard had seen it, but if he had, he certainly added his own improvements.

The 'Mason's Confession' is another text of this type, and is usually dated 1727 because it claims to describe Lodge practice of that date; but it was not published until 1756 and Prichard cannot have seen it. Its only value in our present study is that it supports the existence of the 'multiple precautions and penalties' at this period.

The third text in this group is *The Mystery of Free-Masonry*, to which Prichard had referred in *The Author's Vindication of himself* (See notes on pp. 18 above). It had appeared in print on 15 August 1730, and was discussed in Grand Lodge on August 28. On the fragile argument that its Obligation—which he said was 'entirely genuine'—had appeared several times 'in the Publick papers' he considered that his own oath of secrecy was 'abrogated'.

If it was indeed 'genuine', one would have expected Prichard to print it as it stood, but Prichard's version showed a substantial improvement. For the reader's convenience, it is reproduced here for comparison with the version in *Masonry Dissected*, under Q. 24, in the facsimile:

> I Solemnly protest and swear, in the Presence of Almighty God, and this Society, that I will not, by Word of Mouth or Signs, discover any Secrets which shall be communicated to me this Night, or at any time hereafter: That I will not write, carve, engrave, or cause to be written, carved, or engraven the same, either upon Paper, Copper, Brass, Wood, or Stone, or any Moveable or Immoveable, or any other way discover the same, to any but a Brother or Fellow Craft, under no less Penalty than having my Heart pluck'd thro' the Pap of my Left-Breast, my Tongue by the Roots from the Roof of my Mouth, my Body to be Burnt, and my Ashes to be scatter'd abroad in the Wind, whereby I may be lost to the remembrance of a Brother.

It is noteworthy that Prichard, with three degrees, gave a lengthy Obligation in the E.A. degree, and none in the second or third. Thirty years were to pass before we find documents which contain separate Obligations and penalties for all three ceremonies.

FORM AND DIMENSIONS OF THE LODGE.   Q. 25-29

At this point, Prichard's catechism abandons the ceremonial and procedural details and resumes its principal functions of education and explanation. Many of his themes begin with a question that originated in one of the early texts and are developed with materials from some of the later ones. We shall deal only with the more interesting items.

Q. 25. What Form is the Lodge? A. A long Square. This Question was in *The Wilkinson MS.*, c.1727, with the answer 'An Oblong Square'. Prichard's text added four more; How long? How broad? How high? How deep?, with answers of a mildly symbolical character (See Questions 26-29).

Q. 28. The Question 'How high?', goes back to the *Sloane MS.*, c.1700:

(Q.) how high is your Lodge

(A) without foots yards or Inches it reaches to heaven

The Trinity College, Dublin, MS. 1711, enlarges the answer:

A. As high as ye stars inches, & feet innumerable.

The Dumfries No. 4 MS., c. 1710, uses two questions:

Q. how high is your lodge A. inches & spans Inumberable

Q. how Inumberable A. the material heavens & stary firmament

The theme persisted, but the *Wilkinson MS.*, c.1727, abbreviated the answer:

A. Feet & Inches Innumerable

and Prichard, Q. 28, said

A. Inches, Feet and Yards innumberable, as high as the Heavens

LOCATION AND ORIENTATION OF THE LODGE. Q. 30-32

The need for a solitary location for the lodge was expressed in terms which probably varied in different areas. Eight texts, including the earliest, prescribed a site 'without bark of dog or crow of cock'; five of them used the 'Hill-Vale' or 'Hill-Valley' phrase and three of the later versions, 1723-1730, quoted 'the Vale of Jehosaphat'. The words seem to be of operative origin, envisaging lodges held out of town, in some secluded part of the countryside. There is interesting support for this in a By-law of the Lodge of Aberdeen, dated 1670, at a time when the Lodge was still operative, but with a substantial non-operative membership as well. In this case, however, provision was made for bad weather:

> WEE ordaine lykwayes that no lodge be holden within a dwelling house wher ther is people living, in it but in the open fieldes except it be ill weather, and then Let ther be a house chosen that no person shall heir nor see ws

Q. 31 and 32 deal with the orientation of the lodge and the majority of our documents agree 'east and west, as the Temple of Jerusalem' or they say the lodge 'stands East and West as all Temples do', implying the idea of 'Holy ground' which Prichard used in his answer to Q. 30.

(See *A.Q.C.* 83, pp. 346/7).

THREE PILLARS—WISDOM, STRENGTH AND BEAUTY. Q. 33-35

Only one early text had made mention of 'three pillars' in the lodge, the *Dumfries No. 4 MS.*, c.1710, with the statement that they are 'ye square the compas & ye bible'. Prichard's Q. 34 and 35 broke new ground with three pillars that 'support a Lodge' and his answers mark the appearance of a piece of symbolism that has survived in our present-day ritual and Lectures. The *Wilkinson MS*, c.1727, is the only text that has the same answers almost word for word.

FURNITURE AND JEWELS. Q. 37-47

This group of questions and answers dealing with the 'Furniture' and 'Jewels' of the Lodge and their uses, form a catalogue of twelve items in all, listed in four sets of triads. Since none of the earlier documents contains all twelve items, it seems likely that Prichard's list was a composite of several streams of working. In that era of change, the items themselves and their technical names show marked variations, and their classifications differ, so that 'Jewels' in the early texts become 'Furniture' in *Masonry Dissected*. As a result, it becomes difficult to make a precise comparison between Prichard's answers and those of his predecessors. In the following summary, Prichard's twelve are grouped and listed in the order of their appearance, and compared with the nearest corresponding items in the earlier texts:

> Prichard's 'Furniture': Mosaic Pavement; Blazing Star; Indented Tarsel. The latter is defined as the 'Border round about' the Lodge. This is the first appearance of the indented border in our modern Tracing Boards and carpets.
>
> The 'Edinburgh group', 1696-c.1714 ('Jewels'): 'Perpend Esler; Square pavement; broad ovall'. The latter is probably a corruption of *broached ornel*, i.e., a stone that has been worked with a broaching axe.
>
> *Sloane MS.*, c.1700 ('Jewels'): Square pavement; blazing Star; Danty tassley' The latter is probably a corruption of *perpentashlar*, a dressed or hewn stone that extends through a wall from one side to the other, serving as a binding stone.
>
> 'A Mason's Confession' c.1727. ('Jewels'): Square pavement; dinted ashlar; broached dornal, (i.e., broached ornel).

* * *

Prichard's 'Other Furniture': Bible, Compass and Square.

*Dumfries No.4 MS.,c.*1710: 'Square, compas and bible' (but they are called the three pillars that support the lodge).

*Wilkinson MS., c.*1727: 'Bible, Compasses and Square'. (Furniture). Note; none of the other texts contains these three items as a triad.

* * *

Prichard's 'Jewels Moveable': Square, Level and Plumb-Rule.

*Institution of Free Masons, c.*1725: 'Of Square, Plumb & Rule . . .' in answer to a question 'How is it [the Lodge] governed?'

Grand Mystery . . . Discover'd, 1724: 'Of Square and Rule'.

*Wilkinson MS., c.*1727: Square, Level & Plumb.

Note; this triad does not appear in the earlier texts. We shall see below, in the answers to Q.57 and 59, that Prichard's Moveable Jewels were, respectively, the Jewels of the Master and Wardens, apparently of recent introduction.

* * *

Prichard's 'Jewels Immoveable': Trasel Board, Rough Ashlar and Broach'd Thurnel'. The latter is a corruption of broached ornel.

*Wilkinson MS., c.*1727: 'Mosaick Pavement, dented Asler and broached Urnell'. The first item is mis-named and the text explains that 'the Mosaick Pavement [is] for the Master to draw his design upon', i.e., it serves the same purpose as Prichard's Trasel Board.

Note, none of the other texts contains this triad.

This completes Prichard's catalogue of Furniture and Jewels, all of which have survived, with suitable explanations, in our present-day Lectures.

LIGHTS AND FIX'D LIGHTS. Q. 48-55

The 'Lights' questions go back to the 'Edinburgh group', with answers indicating that they were windows or natural lights in 'The Northeast, the Southwest, & the Eastern passage'. All three texts in this group say that the lights 'denote' the Master, Warden (?), and Fellow Craft. I suggest that the second item is 'warden', as given in the *E.R.H. MS.*; but the *C.C. MS.*, says 'the Words' and the *Kevan MS.*, says 'the word'. The subsequent texts produced many minor variations, but in Prichard's work they become three 'fix'd Lights, i.e., windows in the East, South and West 'To light the Men to, at and from their Work.' By this time he has another set of three Lights, i.e., large Candles placed on high Candlesticks (as explained in his N.B. note) and they represent the 'Sun, Moon and Master-Mason.'

These *N.B.* notes are Prichard's own explanatory (and sometimes critical) comments on the text. They show that he was producing his material as he found it, adding his useful explanations where necessary.

SITUATIONS AND DUTIES OF THE OFFICERS. Q. 56-63

The situations and duties of the officers are covered in Q. 56-63. This group of questions has already been mentioned on p. 28 above as an example of the expansion of the ritual between 1696 and 1730. The answers to Q. 57 and Q. 59 contain interesting passages, printed in italics in Prichard's version, which appear to be his own additional notes, and they probably formed no part of the spoken answers when recited in Lodge.

There was apparently no formal Opening and Closing of Lodges in Prichard's day, and it is interesting to note that thirty years later, most of the questions in this group (after suitable modification and embellishment) were embodied in the ceremony of Opening a Lodge, as shown in another exposure, *Three Distinct Knocks*, 1760.

SECRETS—THE TONGUE OF GOOD REPORT. Q. 65-71

Prichard's Q. 65-71 are directly related to a set of questions in the 'Edinburgh group' of texts, 1696—*c*.1714, and similar questions appear in most of our docmuents; but Prichard enlarges on the answers, and he adds an N.B. note to explain items that might be obscure. Incidentally, the 'tongue of good report' goes back to the *Sloane MS.*, *c*.1700.

GEOMETRY. Q. 72-74

Q. 72 to 74 are a kind of miniature lesson in Geometry, and we shall find more of this in the *Fellow-Craft's* DEGREE. All the *Old*

Charges, from the earliest operative times, spoke in praise of Geometry, the fifth and principal science, often explaining that it is the most important of all the Seven Liberal Arts and Sciences, because it is the foundation of Masonry.

The Wilkinson MS., c.1727, contains the same answers as Prichard's for Q. 72 and 73, but in reply to Q. 74, its answer is headed:

Definitions in Euclid

followed by four definitions.

'The ₁Mason's Examination', 1723, and *The Mystery of Free-Masonry,* 1730, both have a question on the number of Orders in Architecture, and the Five Orders are listed in the reply; but this question is expanded in the *Grand Mystery of Free-Masons Discover'd,* 1724 (and a sister text of c.1725) where we are told that:

A. They answer to the Base, Perpendicular, Diameter, Circumference, and Square.

and we are back to Geometry again. It is noteworthy, however, that these geometrical notes do not occur in the six earliest catechisms. It is only in the later documents, five in all, that we find these elementary pieces, more-or-less closely related to Geometry, and taken together they seem to represent *a Speculative effort* to maintain and enlarge on the operative attachment to Geometry.

PRINCIPAL SIGNS. Q. 75-77

Q. 75 to 77 provide four titles describing the principal modes of recognition in those days, but without any precise details. They may have been test questions, but the same four titles made their first appearance, *without any questions,* in the *Grand Mystery of Free-Masons Discover'd,* 1724, which added four inexplicable diagrams. The titles were also catalogued in the *Institution of Free Masons,* c.1725 (a sister text to the *Grand Mystery . . .*) but again without any questions.

MISCELLANEOUS QUESTIONS. Q. 78-84

Q. 78 and 79 explain the difference between Operative and Gentlemen-Masons. A slightly abbreviated version appears in the *Wilkinson MS.,* c.1727, all in a single Q. and A.

Q. 80 and 81 are evidently a pair of trap questions and Prichard's N.B. note explains the 'Yellow and Blue'. The same Q. and A. appear in the *Dumfries MS. c.* 1710 and in the *Wilkinson MS., c.* 1727. In *The Mason's Confession, c.*1727, the question is 'What's a mason's livery?' and the answer 'A yellow cap and blue breeches, meaning the compasses.' Prichard's answer also appears in the *Mystery of Freemasonry*, 1730, a text that was well known to him.

Q. 83 and 84. These are probably test questions and Prichard offers no explanations. The Chalk and Charcoal were used for 'Drawing the Lodge', i.e. the crude pictorial representations of the Tools, Emblems, etc., which were the earliest versions of the modern 'Tracing Board'. The symbolism 'Freedom, Fervency and Zeal' is preserved in the French exposures as 'Freedom, Constancy and Zeal; but the *Trahi* (instead of Chalk, Charcoal and Earthen Pan) says 'Lime or Mortar, Spade and Brick', still giving them the same symbolism.

The 'Earthen Pan' is a mystery. It appears as *terrine* in several French exposures in the 1740s, which described how an earthern pan filled with live coals was prepared in the Lodge room. At the moment of the Candidate's admission, powdered resin was thrown on to the coals, causing a terrifying flare, to frighten him. But there is no evidence of any such practice in England in Prichard's day.

Two Pillars for the E.A.—Lettering.   Q. 85-87

Q. 85 to 87. Here, in the course of three questions and answers, Prichard deals with important elements of the E.A. ceremony of his day and his N.B. notes are very useful, as always.

We have already noted, in surveying the earliest ritual texts, from 1696-*c.*1714 (i.e. the 'Edinburgh group', on pp. 23-24 above) that they depict the two-degree system of that period. Two pillar-names were then associated with the E.A. ceremony, and the Points of Fellowship were in the second degree.

There is good evidence in *The Whole Institutions . . . Opened*, 1725, and the *Graham MS.*, 1726, that the pillar-names were sometimes used separately, either in the course of a greeting, or a test, when one Brother would say J., and B. was 'the answer to it'; but throughout the two-degree texts, both pillar-names belonged to the E.A.

Prichard, *in his trigradal exposure*, still gave two pillars to the E.A., and explained how one of them was 'lettered'. This was not his own invention; the same details had appeared in print in the *Mystery of Free-Masonry*, 1730, only two months before. We shall return shortly to this subject when dealing with Prichard's *Fellow-Craft's* DEGREE.

In these three questions, Prichard resumes the 'Exam'. and 'Resp'. headings (as used in Q. 8 to 10) clearly indicating something special or unusual, though it is not easy to explain why those questions should be distinguished in this manner. All these 'Exam.-Resp'. questions are in harmony with our earliest texts (if not directly descended from them) so that the headings 'Exam'. and 'Resp'. do not indicate *new* material. It seems possible that the questions marked in this way were not reserved for use by the Master and candidate, but were rehearsed by two selected Brethren on evenings when there was no candidate and therefore no need for the normal full-length catechism.

MISCELLANEOUS QUESTIONS. Q. 88-92

The *Enter'd 'Prentice*'s DEGREE ends with a block of five questions (Q. 88-92) which seem to be rather aimless, but were probably used for test purposes.

The 'Day and Night' questions appear in manuscripts of *c.*1710, 1711, and *c.*1727 (*E.M.C.* pp. 63, 70, 138) with two versions in print, in 1723 and 1726 (*E.M.C.* pp. 74.98).

The 'Wind' question appears in 1711, and again in *c.*1727 (*E.M.C.* pp. 70, 137).

The 'Clock' question appeared in print in 1724, and in manuscripts of *c.*1725 and *c.*1727 (*E.M.C.* pp. 77, 83, 137)

The 'How old' question appears only in two of the later documents and they do not agree, although both texts are clearly designed to indicate a Mason's status. *The Wilkinson MS.*, *c.*1727, says:

> ... Apprentice under Seven; fellow Craft under 14; When a Master, three times Seven.

The Mystery of Free-Masonry, 1730, says:

Q. How old are you?

A. Under 5, or under 7, which you will.

N.B. When you are first made a Mason, you are only entered Apprentice; and till you are made a Master, or, as they call it pass'd the Master's Part, you are only an enter'd Apprentice, and consequently must answer under 7; for if you say above, they will expect the Master's Word and Signs.

* * *

This completes our examination of Prichard's *Enter'd 'Prentice's Degree*, in which we have been mainly concerned to show how strongly his text was based on materials, or on sources that go back, in many instances, to the earliest ritual texts that have survived. If he was, or had been, a Freemason, nothing could justify his breach of the Obligation; the only point that can be made in his favour is that in this ceremony, at least, he was not inventing new material.

FELLOW-CRAFT'S DEGREE

Prichard's F.C. degree contains no details of 'preparation' or 'floorwork', so that, apart from two questions relating to the modes of recognition, it is impossible to reconstruct the actual details of the admission procedure. The text is an extraordinary mixture of materials, old and new, educational rather than ceremonial. There are only thirty-two questions in all, including five long Q. & A. in verse, which deal mainly with the Letter G, and make up about one-third of the whole. They will be examined in sequence, as hitherto, with additional notes on individual points that demand special attention.

In dealing with Prichard's *Fellow-Craft's Degree* and his *Master's Degree*, we find many items for which there is no parallel in the early texts, and this deprives us of the principal check that we may have as to whether he was describing the practices of his own day, or simply inventing new material. There is, however, one further check that remains open to us, and that is *the degree of acceptance that Prichard's work achieved in the later documents of this class*. In dealing with *Masonry Dissected*, however, we are strangely hampered, because of the remarkable success that it achieved. During the next thirty years, 1730-1760, apart from regular re-issues of Prichard's work, there were no new exposures of any value published in England. For the intervening period, the thirty-year gap, the most useful information comes from the best of the early

French exposures, which began to appear in 1737, followed in 1738 by a translation of *Masonry Dissected* and a stream of later works, some of them worthless trash, and several of high importance. The best of these were largely based on Prichard's work, but with valuable expansions.

For our present purpose, we select two of the most interesting works:

1. *Le Catéchisme des Francs-Maçons*, 1744, by a well-known journalist, Louis Travenol, writing under the pseudonym Leonard Gabanon. It contained, *inter alia*, a spendid third degree and a catechism covering all three degrees; but the latter was in 'continuous' form, i.e. it was not split up into three separate parts.[1]
2. *L'Ordre des Francs-Maçons Trahi*, 1745, by an unknown writer, a plagiarist, who was willing to steal his material and add his own comments and improvements. His first and second degrees were 'borrowed' from an earlier work of 1742, and they need not concern us here. His third degree and catechism were based on *Le Catéchisme*, with his own additions. The catechism is still 'continuous', with notes indicating the questions that belong to Fellows and to Masters.[1]

For English texts that may serve to show how widely Prichard's material was accepted by later writers, there are two exposures available to us, *Three Distinct Knocks*, 1760, which claims to depict Antients' practice, and *J. & B.*, 1762, which describes Moderns' usage. As regards their ritual contents, the texts are virtually identical, except in relation to the modes of recognition in the E.A. and F.C. degrees, where the latter is believed to reflect changes that had been made by the premier Grand Lodge in the 1730s; but this point is not relevant in our present study. We shall use these four texts as our 'yardstick' in those cases where no earlier documents throw light on Prichard's sources.

It is necessary to emphasize that our study is strictly confined to *Masonry Dissected*, 1730, its sources and authenticity, and in using the later texts from 1744 to 1762, we are trying to determine how

---

[1] See *The Early French Exposures* (E.F.E.) which contains all twelve of the earliest French texts, 1737-1751, in English translation. Edited and with introductory notes to each text by H. Carr, and published by the Q.C. Lodge.

far Prichard's work was accepted or rejected by contemporary writers in the same field. These notes take no account of the massive accretions and changes that took place in the late 18th and early 19th centuries. We are solely concerned here with Prichard and the ritual of his own period.

THE F.C. CATECHISM. Q. 93

The F.C. catechism begins with a formal question:

Q. 93. Are you a Fellow-Craft? A. I am.

Normally, we would expect the next question to pursue the examination, i.e., 'How shall I know it?' followed by the customary tests. Instead of that, Prichard says:

Q. 94. Why was you made a Fellow-Craft?

A. For the sake of the Letter G.

Q. 95. What does that G. denote?

A. Geometry, or the fifth Science.

GEOMETRY AND THE LETTER G. Q. 94-95

We have already noted (in Q. 72-74 on pp. 88-9 above) what appears to be a Speculative attempt to revive the theme, which recurs constantly in the *Old Charges*, that Geometry is the essential element in Masonry, so that they are virtually synonymous. Here, in Q. 94, 95, which have no parallel in the earliest *ritual texts*, we find it again.

The only English text that uses the Letter G in a somewhat similar manner is the *Wilkinson MS.*, of *c.*1727:

Q. What is the Center of y^r Lodge

A. the Letter G

Q. What does it Signify

A. Geometry

Le Catéchisme repeats Prichard's Q. 94 and 95 word for word (*E.F.E.* p. 105).

The *Trahi* adds various details:

Q. Are you a Fellow?

A. Yes, I am.

Q. How were you made a Fellow?

A. By the Square, the Letter G., & the Compasses
 An allusion to the three steps which the Candidate is made to take.

Q. Why were you made a Fellow?

A. For [the sake of] the Letter G.

Q. What does that Letter signify?

A. Geometry, or the fifth Science (*E.F.E.* p. 264)

Trahi furnishes a different answer, to be given when the question is addressed to a M.M., but that is irrelevant here, and we shall deal with it later. The two English exposures, *T.D.K.* and *J. & B.* do not have these questions.

We shall see, later on, that the Letter G has two meanings, but, in Prichard's text, the subject of Geometry is temporarily abandoned for new themes that have no links with the earlier documents.

TRAVEL, WORK, WAGES—THE MIDDLE CHAMBER. Q. 96-99 & 107-109

Q. 96. Did you ever travel?

A. Yes. East and West

Q. 97. Did you ever work?

A. Yes, in the Building of the Temple.

Q. 98. Where did you receive your Wages?

A. In the middle Chamber

Prichard's travel question, Q. 96, is particularly interesting, because of the speculative interpretation which the French exposures give to it.

Le Catéchisme, Q. How do Apprentice-Fellows travel?

A. From West to East

Q. Why?

A. To seek the Light

This last Q. and A. is a typical piece of French symoblism appended to English ritual. A great deal of Prichard's material from all three degrees will be found in the French documents, often with symbolic expansions that did not yet exist in the English forms. Incidentally, *Le Catéchisme* says that Masters (i.e. M.M.'s.) travel from E. to W., 'To spread the Light'. The *Trahi* has almost identical questions and answers. They are not in *T.D.K.* or *J. & B.*

Prichard's Q. 97, 98, 107 to 109, on Work, Wages, the Middle Chamber and the Winding Stair, are all paraphrased in *Le Catéchisme,* in a series of questions apparently addressed to the M.M., who says that he worked 'in the Middle Chamber' and that the Winding Stair rose by 'three, five & seven'. (*E.F.E.* p. 109). The *Trahi* re-arranges the questions and it is the E.A. who enters the Temple by a Winding Stair (*E.F.E.* p. 261) and the M.M. who works and receives his wages in the Middle Chamber (*E.F.E.* p. 265). *T.D.K.* and *J. & B.* have the F.C.'s working in the Building of the Temple and receiving their wages 'In the middle Chamber'; but both texts omit the Winding Stair.

THE PILLARS—THEIR DIMENSIONS AND ORNAMENTATION. Q. 100-106

Questions 100 to 106. The Pillars in the Porch of K.S.T. have their place in all the early catechisms and exposures, but their architectural and ornamental details appear for the first time in a Masonic context in *Masonry Dissected* and those details are preserved in all four texts, *Catéchisme, Trahi, T.D.K.* and *J. & B.*

TESTS FOR ADMISSION TO THE MIDDLE CHAMBER. Q. 110-117

Questions 110 to 117 deal with the Candidate's symbolic admission into the Middle Chamber, and what he is supposed to have seen there; but this little group of questions touches on several different themes. The first three, Q. 110-112, describe the examination prior to admission, but there are no precedents for these procedures, because Prichard's text is the earliest description we have of a newly-evolving ceremony. We shall touch on this subject under 'THE F.C. PILLAR' on pp. 99-101 below.

Q. 113 appears to be a catch question, not easily explained.

RELIGIOUS SIGNIFICANCE OF THE LETTER 'G'. Q. 114-117

Q. 114-117 are a group of questions leading, first of all, to the Letter G, with its new meaning 'GOD'. *Le Catéchisme*, in spite of its earlier definition of the Letter G, for Geometry, also contains questions which lead to the new meaning:

Q. And after you had entered [the Middle Chamber] What did you see?

A. A great Light, in which I perceived the Letter G.

Q. What does the Letter G signify?

A. God [sic] which means *Dieu*, or [one who is] greater than you. (*E.F.E.* p. 109)

The *Trahi*, in a series of similar Questions addressed to 'a Fellow', says that the Letter G signifies Geometry; but it adds a note to that answer:

> *If it is a Master who is being asked the meaning of the* Letter G, *he replies*: A thing greater than you.
> *Question:* What can this thing be which is greater than I, who am a Free-Mason & Master?
> *Answer:* GOD [sic] which (*en Anglois*) means *Dieu*
> (*E.F.E.* p. 264)

The use of the English word 'God' in two French texts is ample proof of their English origins and we shall see, shortly, that the enlarged answers in *Trahi* were not a French invention, but copied almost *verbatim* from Prichard's Q. 115 and 116:

Q. 115. Who doth that G denote?

A. One that's greater than you.

Q. 116. Who's greater than I, that am a Free and Accepted Mason, the Master of a Lodge?

[97]

A.   The Grand Architect & Contriver of the Universe, or He that was taken up to the top of the Pinnacle of the Holy Temple.

These two answers are particularly interesting, because they made their first appearance (in somewhat embryonic form) in the *Sloane MS.*, as early as *c.*1700:

Q. from whome do you derive your principalls

A. from a great^{er} than you

Q. who is that on earth that is great^{er} than a freemason

A. he y^t was caryed to ye highest pinnicall of the Temple of Jerusalem

(*E.M.C.* p. 47)

Sloane speaks of 'a freemason' and Prichard adds 'the Master of a Lodge', and it is strange to find this purely Christian theme of Christ on the pinnacle of the Temple (Matthew, 4, v.5 and Luke 4, v.9) being used simply to emphasize their greatness. It is difficult to understand why Prichard was at pains to retain this item which had apparently disappeared from all the intervening texts between *c.*1700 and 1730 and this seems to suggest that these questions were still in general use, at least in Prichard's own circle. This view is supported by the two French texts, which preserved the tenor of the questions even though they discarded the 'pinnacle' theme. (Prichard's Q.115 and 116 are not to be found in *T.D.K.* or *J. & B.*)

GEOMETRY AGAIN.   Q. 117-121

From Q.117 to the end of the F.C. degree, the questions are headed, 'Exam'. and 'Resp.', and *The Repeating of the Letter G* is conducted in the form of quatrains, suggesting that it was recited by two Brethren specially briefed for that purpose. The emphasis, in this section, is on G for Geometry, and the response to Q. 121 is a paraphrase of the 'geometrical' answer to Q. 74 in the *Enter'd Prentice's Degree*.

A GREETING.   Q. 122-125

Q. 122 to 125: the four final questions seem to represent a formalised manner of conveying the 'greeting', each line spoken by the 'Examiner' demanding the correct reply from the 'Responder'. Needless to say, the 'greeting' appears in most of the early catechisms and exposures from 1696 onwards.

THE F.C. PILLAR. Q. 112

Q. 112. Prichard adds a very useful N.B. note to this question, but the most interesting aspect of the answer is the manner in which he allocated the pillar-names to the E.A. and F.C. We have already seen (in Q. 86 and 87) that he had preserved the early practice in giving two pillars to the E.A. Here, in Q. 112, he used the second pillar again, this time for the F.C., and we have no means of checking the accuracy of this arrangement, because *Masonry Dissected* was unique in this respect; there is no other text that used the pillar-names in the same way. This involves a very interesting aspect of the evolution of the three-degree system, which is—in many aspects—one of the major unsolved problems of Masonic history.

We shall deal with the third degree in due course. For the present we are only concerned with the evidence relating to the use of the pillar-names in the texts that preceded Prichard's work, and in some of the French and English texts that followed it.

A survey of all the texts that were written or published before Prichard's work appeared in 1730, reveals that, with only one exception and despite variations in usage, all of them allocated two pillars for the E.A. The exception is the *Trinity College, Dublin, MS.*, of 1711, which divided various signs, words, etc., into *three groups*, for the E.A., F.C., and Master. It was apparently an early sketch of trigradal procedure, and it gave B. to the E.A., and J. to the F.C.[2] To avoid misunderstanding it must be noted that there is positively no evidence of the three degrees being actually in practice at this early date, 1711. A similar division of the pillar-names appears in the *Mason's Confession*, supposedly representing procedures of 1727, but that text was not published until 1756 and is therefore irrelevant in the present question.

---

[2] *The Wilkinson MS.*, c.1727, may also be mentioned here. It gives the B., 'lettered' and 'halved', to the E.A. The J. pillar is only mentioned in a Biblical marginal note; it does not appear anywhere in the catechism itself, so that it affords no useful evidence on the present question.

If we are to use post-Prichard texts as a means of judging how far his work was accepted by later writers in this field, we shall find that none of them followed his arrangement of two pillars for the E.A., and J alone for the F.C. A summary of later procedures shows, quite definitely, that when the trigradal system had settled down into general use, there remained only one pillar for the E.A., and the other for the F.C. Even so, there was one interesting variation caused largely by the fact that the English Grand Lodge—at some stage between 1730 and 1739—had reversed the sequence of the words. It is not surprising, therefore, to find that the best of the French exposures use the pillar-names in what might be described as 'reverse order', e.g.

> *Le Secret des Francs-Maçons*, 1742, has J. for the Apprentice and B. for the Fellow, both 'lettered'. *Le Catéchisme* . . . 1744, the *Trahi*, 1745, *La Désolation.* . . . , 1747, and *Le Maçon Démasqué*, 1751, all follow the same procedure.

Incidentally, and while on the subject of 'reverse order', the *Trahi* (*L'Ordre des Francs-Maçons Trahi*), 1745, was the first of all the exposures to include details of 'Passwords' which, according to the anonymous author, had been then recently introduced as an additional safeguard for the Masons, when dealing with Brethren 'whom they do not know'. Masonic 'Passwords' were unknown in Prichard's day, and when they make their first appearance in print in the *Trahi* and in subsequent French texts, they are also in 'reverse order', which suggests that they may have been of English or Irish origin. There is a record in the Inquisition documents at Lisbon in 1738 which might support that theory. (*A.Q.C.* 84 p. 93)

At the end of the thirty-year gap in the English texts, *Three Distinct Knocks*, in 1760, purported to describe the procedure of Lodges working under the 'Antients', the rival Grand Lodge (established in 1751) which had rejected the changes introduced by the older body. This was reflected in *T.D.K.*, which gave B. to the E.A., and permitted both 'lettering' and 'halving', though the catechism only 'halved' the word. It gave J. to the F.C., neither 'halved' nor 'lettered', and 'Passwords' were embodied in the text in 'reverse order'.

J. & B. appeared in 1762, claiming to represent the usage of the premier Grand Lodge. It gave J. to the E.A., with the option of 'halving' or 'lettering', but the text only 'halved' the word: it gave B. to the F.C., again, neither 'lettered' nor 'halved', and it also contained 'Passwords' which were, in this instance, in agreement with *T.D.K*.

To return to *Masonry Dissected*, having examined the principal ritual documents that followed its publication, we are inevitably driven to the conclusion that Prichard was describing the pillar-name procedures *at an intermediate stage of development*. He may have been recounting the practice in one particular Lodge, or in a small group of lodges, before the later arrangement of one pillar for each of the first two degrees had become widely accepted.

Before closing this section on the F.C. Degree, it is important to stress that the second degree of the trigradal system was achieved by a separation of the original first degree into two parts, each having one of the pillar-names as its central theme. Prichard showed how the new and rather slender second degree was amplified by the Middle Chamber materials and the Letter G. In later developments it acquired further additions, i.e., the Lectures on the Five Senses and on the Orders of Architecture, the latter being an expansion of lists of the Five Orders in several of the early texts; but these items are beyond our present study.

THE MASTER'S DEGREE

Prichard's *Master's* Degree or *Master's Part* is in the form of a catechism of only thirty questions and answers, and apart from the 'Points of Fellowship' and the 'Entrusting' it contains no hint of 'floorwork' or ceremonial procedure. It begins with a set of three questions which, since they refer to the third degree, have no precise parallel in the earlier texts. The answer to Q. 126 contains the now familiar "try me, prove me. . . . .".

God And The Square.

Q. 129.　How came you to be pass'd Master?

A.　　　By the help of God, the Square and my own Industry.

This answer is of special interest because the words 'God and the Square' are clearly related to a wide variety of questions in the earlier documents. None of the three texts in the 'Edinburgh group', 1696—*c*.1714, had questions on this point; but in each of them, the E.A's and F.C's, on their return to the Lodge, recited the 'words of entrie', which contained:

> .....As I am sworn by God and St. Jhon by the Square and Compass...
>
> (E.M.C. p. 33)

Here, the link is very faint, but it is much stronger in the later versions:

> *Sloane MS., c.*1700. Q. What were you sworne by
> A. by god and the Square
>
> (E.M.C. p. 48)

In *The Whole Institution of Masonry*, 1724, and in *The Whole Institutions of Free-Masons Opened*, 1725:

[Q] Whoe is Master of all Lodge's

[A] God and the Square

> (E.M.C. pp. 81, 87)

In *The Grand Mystery Laid Open*, 1726

[Q] Who is your Founder

[A] God and the Square

[Q] By what Oath did you Swear to conceal the secret Word?

[A] By God, the Square, the King, and the Master.

> (E.M.C. pp. 97, 98).

The *Graham MS*, 1726, is unique in many respects, not least because its compiler framed much of his material with 'Some Referance to Scripture'. In explanation of the words "poor and penyless blind and Ignorant. . . ." he wrote:

> ... in regard our saviour became poor ffor our redemption so I became poor at that time for the knowledge of God contracted in the square
>
> (E.M.C. p. 90)

This was probably an allusion to the candidate's posture in the Obligation, i.e., kneeling on the floor within the arms of a large square. Later, in explanation of the duties implicit in the Mason's obligation, he wrote:

> . . . to obey God and all true Squares made or sent from a brother . . .
>
> . . . never to steall Least I should ofend God and shame the square
>
> (*E.M.C.* p. 91)

Prichard's Q. 130. How was you pass'd Master?

    A.   From the Square to the Compass

There is no comparable question in the earlier texts, but the *Wilkinson MS.*, c.1727, a contemporary of Prichard has a closely related question which deserves attention:

Q. if a Mason be lost where is he to be found

A. Between the Square & the Compass

                                        (*E.M.C.* p. 138)

The *Wilkinson* question and answer were regularly repeated in the best of the French exposures. Prichard's answer seems to imply that the Square belonged to the F.C., and the Compass to the M.M., and both answers find a measure of support in the French texts.

Le Catéchisme, 1744, was the first work that contained illustrations of the Tracing Boards. There was one entitled 'Plan of the Apprentice-Fellow's Lodge', i.e. a combined T.B. for both E.A. and F.C. The other was a 'Plan of the Master's Lodge' (See *E.F.E.* p. 99). Its central theme is a kind of coffin design, drawn with head towards the West and Foot towards the East. At the western end of the coffin is a large square, its arms pointing westwards; at the eastern end is a pair of open compasses, also with arms pointing westwards. The design shows, in faint diagram, three curious zig-zag steps, and both the text and illustration indicate that in the M.M. ceremony, the candidate began his advance towards the Master with toes touching the extremities of the square (thus forming a square) and finished with toes touching the points of the compasses, i.e., he travelled 'from the Square to the Compass'. The same design, with even better art-work, was repeated in *Trahi* and in many later French texts. It is impossible to say whether this procedure was followed in Prichard's day, but it does explain his answer to Q. 130, 'From the Square to the Compass'.

THE ESSENCE OF THE THIRD DEGREE. Q. 131-155

From Q. 131 up to the end of the Master's Part, all but two of the questions and answers are headed 'Ex.' and 'R', for no obvious reason. This body of twenty-five questions with some very lengthy answers comprises the essence of the third degree of those days, most of it entirely new material that had not been published before. It seems likely that all these items marked 'Ex.' and 'R', were borrowed from some source outside the traditional materials on which Prichard's E.A. and F.C. degrees were based. Generally, his use of so much material that can be shewn to have been in existence in Masonic ritual for many years before he published *Masonry Dissected*, tends to support the view that he had not invented this new material. This suggests that Prichard had borrowed or adapted those sections from one of the newly developing workings of the third degree, and used the headings 'Ex.' and 'R', simply to distinguish them.

DOGGEREL VERSE. Q. 131, 132

Q. 131 and 132, the first two items in this block of new material, are in doggerel rhyme, lifted bodily from 'The Mason's Examination', 1723, the first printed exposure. The original verses are reproduced here, with Prichard's amended version, which he had framed roughly in the form of question and answer under the headings 'Ex.' and 'R'.

The Mason's Examination, 1723

An enter'd Mason I have been,
Boaz and *Jachin* I have seen;
A Fellow I was sworn most rare,
And know the Astler, Diamond, and Square:
I know the Master's Part full well,
As honest *Maughbin* will you tell.

Then the Master says;
If a Master-Mason you would be,
Observe you well the *Rule of Three*;
And what you want in Masonry,
Thy *Mark* and *Maughbin* makes thee free.

Prichard's Q. 131 and 132

[Q. 131] Ex. An enter'd 'Prentice I presume you have been.
R. *Jachin* and *Boaz* I have seen;
A Master-Mason I was made most rare,
With Diamond, Ashler and the Square.

[Q. 132] Ex. If a Master-Mason you would be,
You must rightly understand the Rule of Three.
And * M.B. shall make you free:
And what you want in Masonry,
Shall in this Lodge be shewn to thee.
R. Good Masonry I understand;
The Keys of all Lodges are all at my Command.
* Machbenah

There seems to be no real reason to explain why Prichard used this material, which had appeared in only one other text. If it had been in wide general use there would surely have been some trace of it in one or more of the other texts. It is difficult to theorize on this kind of problem, but we have already noted on p. 27 above that it is possible to arrange the early texts in several groups which may be taken to represent separate streams of ritual. Prichard's action in preserving these verses may imply that although they had only appeared once before, in 1723, they were probably more widely known in the Craft than that single appearance would suggest.

THE RULE OF THREE. Q. 132

This is a puzzle, because there is no real clue as to *what it meant in Prichard's day*. There are, of course, innumerable modern interpretations.

THE KEYS OF ALL LODGES... Q. 132

The last line of Prichard's verse appears to be his own expansion. Most of the earlier catechisms and exposures contain groups of questions on 'The Key of the Lodge', which fall broadly into two groups:

(i) Those which ask 'Where is it hidden?' or 'How far from the Lodge door?'.
(ii) Those which refer to the theme of secrecy, i.e., a 'well-hung tongue', or to 'the tongue of good report'.

Prichard had used these themes in his E.A. degree, Q.68-71. But all these versions related to a single key, and a single Lodge. In the rhyme, however, the reference is to 'the Keys of all Lodges', implying perhaps that the doors of every Lodge are open to Master Masons.

M.B. Q. 132

The most interesting items in Prichard's verses are the initials M.B. and the footnoted word 'Machbenah', which appears here unexplained, in anticipation of its subsequent appearance at the end of his *Master's Part*. It had appeared in the *Sloane MS. c.* 1700, and in three later versions, all so sadly debased that it would be impossible to say which, if any of them, is correct: this applies also to Prichard's version. One of those texts, *The Whole Institutions of Free-Masons Opened,* 1725, gives the words 'Magboe and Boe' which are said to signify 'Marrow in the Bone', but that may be only a mnemonic. The *Graham MS*, 1726, uses the words 'marrow in this bone', but that phrase may also have been a mnemonic. In every case, the word or its mnemonic was more or less directly associated with the Points of Fellowship.

LOST AND IS NOW FOUND. Q. 135-146

As the earliest version of a degree which was very slowly coming into practice, it is not surprising to find some inconsistencies in the details. One, in particular, relates to the answers to Q. 135 and Q. 136 which state that the Master-Mason's Word 'was lost and is now found'. The words 'now found' do not agree with the story as told in answer to Q. 145, which says that the searchers, *of their own accord*, decided to adopt a substitute word 'if they could not find the Word in him or about him'. At best, it was only the substitute that was 'found', not the original. Incidentally, the same answer, later in the text, suggests that the first words uttered by the searchers at the exhumation were "*Muscus Domus* etc", which implies that certain M.B. details have been accidentally omitted from the text at this point.

The searchers, in Prichard's text (Q.145) were 'Fifteen Loving Brothers' possibly to be identified with the fifteen Fellowcrafts subsequently ordered to attend the funeral (Q.146). If the searchers were indeed Fellowcrafts, they would not know the Word, and were not entitled to know it. That might explain why they resolved to seek 'the Word in him or about him', though in so doing they could have been guilty of a Masonic misdemeanor. (It is always difficult to find logical explanations for legends).

There are no texts of the 1730s with which we can compare Prichard's version. The earliest comparable documents are *le Catéchisme*, 1744, and the *Trahi*, 1745. These two texts—and several later ones—all agree that 'Jehovah' was *'the former Word of a Master'* [i.e. M.M.]. Indeed, that 'Ineffable Name' was regularly embodied, in Hebrew or English characters, on the coffin-design in most of the illustrations of the French third-degree Tracing Boards of that period.

The French texts display considerable improvements on Prichard's version in several respects. They give a complete narrative account of the actual procedure, floorwork, etc., in such detail that it is possible to reconstruct the whole ceremony. Although the elements of the English and French versions of the legend were virtually identical, the French stories were in much more logical detail. For example, there is no mention of the Word that was 'lost and is now found'. Solomon 'ordered *nine Masters* to go in search', in three parties of three. After discovering the corpse and

> . . . having recognized their Master, they surmised that this outrage had been committed by some Fellows, while trying to force him to give them the Master's Word; & fearing that they might have extorted the Word from him, they immediately resolved to change it & to adopt the first word that any of them might utter while disinterring the corpse.
> (E.F.E. pp. 250, 257/8: see also pp. 97/8, 331, 355, 451/4)

These men were Masters and they were not seeking the Master's Word; they knew it. *They only decided to adopt a substitute word out of fear that the assassins had compelled their victim to divulge it.*

[This text appeared in the original printing]

Emblem on Front Cover

Pierced Silver Jewel, 1811, by Thomas Harper, jeweller, of Fleet Street, London, a fine example of many different designs that were produced around the end of the 18th century.

Harper (b.1736, d.1832) was initiated in a Lodge under the 'Antients' Grand Lodge, and eventually became Deputy Master of that body. He also served the Office of Grand Steward of the premier Grand Lodge, the 'Moderns', but was expelled by them in 1803, because of his failure to arrange a fusion of the rival Grand Lodges. There is ample evidence that he did not favour the merger, which was not achieved until 1813.

Colophon

◇◇

Masonry Dissected

◇◇

PRICHARD—CARR

Nine hundred ninety-nine copies of this limited edition were manufactured by Pantagraph Printing Company and Bloomington Offset Process, Inc. of Bloomington, Illinois, the former doing the composition and binding and the latter the presswork.

The type faces used are of the Linotype Janson and Monotype Garamond families. The facsimile pages were reproduced from photographs of a first edition of Prichard, now in the Library of the Grand Lodge of Massachusetts.

The text paper is seventy pound basis radiant white Artemis Text manufactured by the Mohawk Paper Mills, Inc. The book covers are made of Columbia Mills' Riverside Vellum over board and stamped in gold.

All volumes of The Masonic Book Club series are designed and prepared by Louis L. Williams, Alphonse Cerza and Fred A. Dolan.

Related Titles from Westphalia Press

Ancient Mysteries and Modern Masonry: The Collected Writings of Jewel P. Lightfoot, Edited by Billy J. Hamilton Jr.

Jewel P. Lightfoot. Former Attorney General of the State of Texas. Past Grand Master of the Masonic Grand Lodge of Texas. From humble beginnings in rural Arkansas, he worked to become an educated man who excelled in law and Freemasonry. He was a gentleman of his time, well-known as a scholar, public speaker, and Masonic philosopher.

Essay on The Mysteries and the True Object of The Brotherhood of Freemasons
by Jason Williams

This isn't a reprint of a classic. It's a new rendition with new life breathed into it, to be enjoyed both by the layperson trying to understand the Craft and Masonic scholars taking a deeper dive into the fraternity's golden years—when the concepts of liberty and equality were still fresh.

Female Emancipation and Masonic Membership:
An Essential Collection
By Guillermo De Los Reyes Heredia

Female Emancipation and Masonic Membership: An Essential Combination is a collection of essays on Freemasonry and gender that promotes a transatlantic discussion of the study of the history of women and Freemasonry and their contribution in different countries.

Freemasonry, Heir to the Enlightenment
by Cécile Révauger

Modern Freemasonry may have mythical roots in Solomon's time but is really the heir to the Enlightenment. Ever since the early eighteenth century freemasons have endeavored to convey the values of the Enlightenment in the cultural, political and religious fields, in Europe, the American colonies and the emerging United States.

Freemasonry: A French View
by Roger Dachez and Alain Bauer

Perhaps one should speak not of Freemasonry but of Freemasonries in the plural. In each country Masonic historiography has developed uniqueness. Two of the best known French Masonic scholars present their own view of the worldwide evolution and challenging mysteries of the fraternity over the centuries.

Worlds of Print: The Moral Imagination of an Informed Citizenry, 1734 to 1839
by John Slifko

John Slifko argues that freemasonry was representative and played an important role in a larger cultural transformation of literacy and helped articulate the moral imagination of an informed democratic citizenry via fast emerging worlds of print.

Why Thirty-Three?: Searching for Masonic Origins
by S. Brent Morris, PhD

What "high degrees" were in the United States before 1830? What were the activities of the Order of the Royal Secret, the precursor of the Scottish Rite? A complex organization with a lengthy pedigree like Freemasonry has many basic foundational questions waiting to be answered, and that's what this book does: answers questions.

The Great Transformation: Scottish Freemasonry 1725-1810
by Dr. Mark C. Wallace

This book examines Scottish Freemasonry in its wider British and European contexts between the years 1725 and 1810. The Enlightenment effectively crafted the modern mason and propelled Freemasonry into a new era marked by growing membership and the creation of the Grand Lodge of Scotland.

Getting the Third Degree: Fraternalism, Freemasonry and History
Edited by Guillermo De Los Reyes and Paul Rich

As this engaging collection demonstrates, the doors being opened on the subject range from art history to political science to anthropology, as well as gender studies, sociology and more. The organizations discussed may insist on secrecy, but the research into them belies that.

A Place in the Lodge: Dr. Rob Morris, Freemasonry and the Order of the Eastern Star
by Nancy Stearns Theiss, PhD

Ridiculed as "petticoat masonry," critics of the Order of the Eastern Star did not deter Rob Morris' goal to establish a Masonic organization that included women as members. Morris carried the ideals of Freemasonry through a despairing time of American history.

Brought to Light: The Mysterious George Washington Masonic Cave
by Jason Williams MD

The George Washington Masonic Cave near Charles Town, West Virginia, contains a signature carving of George Washington dated 1748. This book painstakingly pieces together the chronicled events and real estate archives related to the cavern in order to sort out fact from fiction.

Dudley Wright: Writer, Truthseeker & Freemason
by John Belton

Dudley Wright (1868-1950) was an Englishman and professional journalist who took a universalist approach to the various great Truths of Life. He travelled though many religions in his life and wrote about them all, but was probably most at home with Islam.

History of the Grand Orient of Italy
Emanuela Locci, Editor

No book in Masonic literature upon the history of Italian Freemasonry has been edited in English up to now. This work consists of eight studies, covering a span from the Eighteenth Century to the end of the WWII, tracing through the story, the events and pursuits related to the Grand Orient of Italy.

westphaliapress.org

Policy Studies Organization

The Policy Studies Organization (PSO) is a publisher of academic journals and book series, sponsor of conferences, and producer of programs.

Policy Studies Organization publishes dozens of journals on a range of topics, such as European Policy Analysis, Journal of Elder Studies, Indian Politics & Polity, Journal of Critical Infrastructure Policy, and Popular Culture Review.

Additionally, Policy Studies Organization hosts numerous conferences. These conferences include the Middle East Dialogue, Space Education and Strategic Applications Conference, International Criminology Conference, Dupont Summit on Science, Technology and Environmental Policy, World Conference on Fraternalism, Freemasonry and History, and the Internet Policy & Politics Conference.

For more information on these projects, access videos of past events, and upcoming events, please visit us at:

www.ipsonet.org

www.ingramcontent.com/pod-product-compliance
Lightning Source LLC
Chambersburg PA
CBHW070044040426
42333CB00041B/2305